Teach Writing to Older Readers Using Picture Books:

Every Picture Tells a Story

BY JANE HEITMAN

Linworth
PUBLISHING, INC

Your Trusted
Library-to-Classroom Connection.
Books, Magazines, and Online.

Library of Congress Cataloging-in-Publication Data

Heitman, Jane.
   Teach writing to older readers using picture books : every picture tells a
story / Jane Heitman.
       p. cm.
   Includes bibliographical references and index.
   ISBN 1-58683-176-3 (pbk.)
   1. Language arts (Secondary) 2. English language—Composition and
exercises—Study and teaching (Secondary) 3. Picture books. I. Title.
LB1631.H35 2004
808'.042'0712—dc22

                          2004018802

Published by Linworth Publishing, Inc.
480 East Wilson Bridge Road, Suite L
Worthington, Ohio 43085

ISBN: 1-58683-176-3

5 4 3 2

Table of Contents

List of Figures

Acknowledgements

A project like this does not come together without the help of many people. Thank you to Amy Armstrong, Linda Armstrong, Lynette Christensen, Maxine Curley, Julia Kleven, Karen McKee, Janet Noland, Connie Parrish, Karen Schniederjan, and Shirley Sternola for their expert advice. Thank you to Olivia Buttars, Jennifer Buechele, and Becky Bernal for professional support. A special thanks to editor Donna Miller, who provided plenty of both.

About the Author

Jane Heitman, author of Linworth's *Rhymes and Reasons: Librarians and Teachers Using Poetry to Foster Literacy*, is a former school teacher and librarian. She has worked in the education field for 25 years and currently manages the interlibrary loan unit at Mesa State College. She has published poetry, curriculum, activities, and other material for children and teachers in church settings. Originally from South Dakota, she now lives in Grand Junction, Colorado, where she volunteers in the children's center at the public library.

Introduction

M y ninth grade English students slogged into the classroom following lunch. They lounged in their seats, nearly nodding off. We attempted to learn story elements and apply them to reading and writing. Unfamiliar terms and grade-level literature worked against comprehension for many of my students. How else could I teach this?

At home, an idea was born when I glanced at my bookshelf. I have never outgrown my love for picture books. The next day I read aloud Marjorie Sharmat's *Sasha the Silly* (New York: Holiday, 1984) to the class. They shifted forward in their chairs, their eyes bright. They grinned at the funny parts, and looked eager to hear the rest of the story. Afterward, the students easily identified characters, plot, setting, and, most nebulous of all, theme. We discussed word choice, style, illustrations (by Janet Stevens), and their effects, and we enjoyed doing it! Another day, I read them Joanna Cole's *Norma Jean, Jumping Bean* (New York: Random, 2003), illustrated by Lyn Munsinger, with the same result. Best of all, they transferred their knowledge to grade-level reading. Students relaxed in their own writing and attempted to employ the techniques we had discussed. Picture books became a regular part of my teaching repertoire and resulted in this book.

Teach Writing to Older Readers Using Picture Books: Every Picture Tells a Story gives tools and strategies to fifth through ninth grade library media specialists and language arts teachers to improve students' writing with the help of picture books.

What is a Picture Book?

Definitions of "picture book" vary. Berthe Amoss and Eric Suben define picture books as those suitable for children aged three to six, that are "usually thirty-two pages in length, that feature artwork on every page and that tell stories through the interaction of art and text" (*The Children's Writer's Reference* 28). *Children's Writer's & Illustrator's Market* says that picture books are "aimed at preschoolers to eight-year-olds" and use a combination of text and artwork to tell a story (348). Children's librarian Julia Kleven considers picture books "something to be read to the very young child" (Julia Kleven. Personal interview. 28 Nov. 2003). In recent years, a number of books have been published containing artwork on every page, but with text and content aimed at older children. *Pink and Say* by Patricia Polacco and *When Marian Sang* by Pamela Muñoz Ryan are two examples. Elementary school librarian Janet Noland reads *Tops and Bottoms* by Janet Stevens to fourth and fifth graders, as she has learned that while younger children like the story, they do not understand the joke (Janet Noland. Personal interview. 28 Nov. 2003.)

For the purposes of this book, the broadest possible definition of "picture book" was applied. Bibliographies include wordless books, indicated with an asterisk (*), as well as books with pictures and text for ages preschool through fifth grade. Books were selected for their quality and appropriateness to their particular chapter. Titles were gathered from the author's personal experience, from library media specialists and teachers, and from reference books and online sources. Editions indicated were in print at the time of this writing. Library binding or hardcover editions were chosen over paperback editions, but many picture books are available in paperback, audiovisual formats, and languages other than English.

Why Use Picture Books?

Picture books' simplicity makes isolating the story element or technique being studied easier. Literary terms and techniques are less intimidating because they are applied to works the students already know or can quickly grasp. Students can then apply what they have learned to more complex literature and writing. Picture books are short enough to read aloud, give a lesson, and write an assignment in one or two class periods. Students can read several books in a class period to apply to their writing assignments.

Picture books are appealing because of their combination of text and pictures. The stories themselves are often charming, touching, or funny. They reach struggling students and excelling students alike.

Do fifth through ninth graders find picture books too babyish? Virginia Mealy says, "The 'baby book' stigma will not be a problem unless the teacher makes it one. When a teacher presents a picture book with genuine enthusiasm and love, who is going to care what the book looks like" (n.p.).

Collaboration

"The school library media specialist can provide strong and creative leadership in building and nurturing this culture of learning, both as a teacher and as an instructional partner" (*Information* 60). As instructional partners, library media specialists are the resource experts for print and non-print material. Connecting students and resources is a challenging, rewarding part of a library media specialist's job. Assisting classroom teachers with their curricular needs strengthens the teachers' lessons.

Library media specialists are also equipped to teach. They have the opportunity to teach research skills one-on-one or in groups. They share their love of reading with students. Library media specialists also plan, design, and conduct lessons in the same way that classroom teachers do.

Teachers are content area experts and know the scope and sequence for their area of study. They know the standards and academic expectations for their areas. They know their students' strengths and weaknesses.

"The library media specialist-teacher team is an educational gift" (Buzzeo, *Collaborating...K-6* 8). Collaboration refers to joint goal setting, planning, and conducting lessons. Roles are defined, expectations are set, and on-going relationships are formed. For more on collaboration, see Bishop, Buzzeo, and *Information Power*.

The activities in this book encourage collaboration between the library media specialist and the language arts teacher. Some activities indicate adding another collaborative partner, such as another content area teacher or special area teacher.

The activities can be conducted wholly by the library media specialist, wholly by the classroom teacher, or with each person leading parts of the lessons. Lessons may be taught in the library, in the classroom, or both.

Teaching Writing

Since both the library media specialist and the classroom teacher may teach the lessons, the following tips apply to both. The leader's role is best described as coach. The leader models, assigns, and does some assessing, but must create a safe, workshop atmosphere where students are free to express themselves in discussion and writing. Asking guiding, open-ended questions helps students discover their own answers. The leader should also be an active reader-writer along with the students and be unafraid to share rough drafts and failed attempts with them.

The leader may create a Reading-Writing Center with areas for groups, individuals, or both. Writing circles are small groups of students who share their work with each other regularly. Many experts recommend that students keep journals and do pre-writing and free-writing activities. Writing circle members develop their revising, editing, and assessment skills. Writing circles also build trust within the group. (See Selected List of Works Consulted, page 134, for more information.)

The leader can model ways to look at literature. The leader should introduce the book to be read, asking students to watch and listen for something particular. Leader-guided discussion between reading and writing prepares students for their writing assignment and builds a bridge between reading and writing. By analyzing published books and researching authors, students learn how professional authors created their stories. They can apply that knowledge to their own writing. Such an approach also reinforces the need to read to be a good writer.

The Activities

The activities in this book, designed for grades five through nine, require little preparation and few supplies. All activities require at least one picture book and student writing materials. Most of these activities can also be completed using basic computer word processing and graphics software. Reproducible templates are included here. Each activity suggests several picture books from which to choose or refers to the chapter bibliography. Each chapter contains a bibliography of picture books pertinent to the chapter's topic. Use them or your own favorites. An asterisk (*) in the bibliographies indicates wordless books. Activities help students model the examples, focus on particular story elements, and write a variety of responses, fiction and nonfiction, in various formats. Activities are intended as starters, which can be modified to accommodate slower or more advanced learners. The lessons are flexible and allow students to engage in higher order thinking skills. If these skills are not explicit in the lesson, they can be added by asking students to analyze or synthesize. Accommodate slower learners by teaching the parts of the lessons that they can grasp. Encourage students to be as creative and thorough as possible. The applicable NCTE standards are listed with each activity, with the full list on page xiv. Activities include technology connections and can be applied to the Six-Trait Writing Assessment Program™.

The Result

Because assessment is so important in today's classroom, a few sample rubrics are included to help teachers and library media specialists develop their own. The rubrics shown apply to single lessons, though the lessons may have several parts. Rubrics can also be developed to apply to projects or several lessons grouped together. Other assessment tools, such as checklists, can also be used. Assessment tools can be used to report students' grades, numeric scores, or progress.

A reading-writing program using picture books develops students' sensitivity to literature, composition, and art. Students will be well prepared for analyzing more difficult literature and writing more complex pieces. They will show greater understanding of story elements in their discussions and written work. And, of course, you and your students will experience the joy of sharing books and stories, your own and other's.

Standards for the Language Arts

SPONSORED BY NCTE AND IRA

The vision guiding these standards is that all students must have the opportunities and resources to develop the language skills they need to pursue life's goals and to participate fully as informed, productive members of society. These standards assume that literacy growth begins before children enter school as they experience and experiment with literacy activities—reading and writing, and associating spoken words with their graphic representations. Recognizing this fact, these standards encourage the development of curriculum and instruction that make productive use of the emerging literacy abilities that children bring to school. Furthermore, the standards provide ample room for the innovation and creativity essential to teaching and learning. They are not prescriptions for particular curriculum or instruction. Although we present these standards as a list, we want to emphasize that they are not distinct and separable; they are, in fact, interrelated and should be considered as a whole.

1. Students read a wide range of print and non-print texts to build an understanding of texts, of themselves, and of the cultures of the United States and the world; to acquire new information; to respond to the needs and demands of society and the workplace; and for personal fulfillment. Among these texts are fiction and nonfiction, classic and contemporary works.

2. Students read a wide range of literature from many periods in many genres to build an understanding of the many dimensions (e.g., philosophical, ethical, aesthetic) of human experience.

3. Students apply a wide range of strategies to comprehend, interpret, evaluate, and appreciate texts. They draw on their prior experience, their interactions with other readers and writers, their knowledge of word meaning and of other texts, their word identification strategies, and their understanding of textual features (e.g., sound-letter correspondence, sentence structure, context, graphics).

4. Students adjust their use of spoken, written, and visual language (e.g., conventions, style, vocabulary) to communicate effectively with a variety of audiences and for different purposes.

5. Students employ a wide range of strategies as they write and use different writing process elements appropriately to communicate with different audiences for a variety of purposes.

6. Students apply knowledge of language structure, language conventions (e.g., spelling and punctuation), media techniques, figurative language, and genre to create, critique, and discuss print and non-print texts.

7. Students conduct research on issues and interests by generating ideas and questions, and by posing problems. They gather, evaluate, and synthesize data from a variety of sources (e.g., print and non-print texts, artifacts, people) to communicate their discoveries in ways that suit their purpose and audience.

8. Students use a variety of technological and information resources (e.g., libraries, databases, computer networks, video) to gather and synthesize information and to create and communicate knowledge.

9. Students develop an understanding of and respect for diversity in language use, patterns, and dialects across cultures, ethnic groups, geographic regions, and social roles.

10. Students whose first language is not English make use of their first language to develop competency in the English language arts and to develop understanding of content across the curriculum.

11. Students participate as knowledgeable, reflective, creative, and critical members of a variety of literacy communities.

12. Students use spoken, written, and visual language to accomplish their own purposes (e.g., for learning, enjoyment, persuasion, and the exchange of information).

Standards for the English Language Arts, by the International Reading Association and the National Council of Teachers of English, Copyright 1996 by the International Reading Association and the National Council of Teachers of English. Reprinted with permission.

CHAPTER 1

Character

C haracter provides the "who" of the story. Memorable characters have distinct personalities, with good and bad traits. Begin your library or classroom study of character by asking students what characters they remember. (If they do not have strong literature backgrounds, allow them to name TV or movie characters.) Then discuss what made those characters memorable.

Point of View

NCTE 1, 3, 6, 11, 12 Point of view means who is telling the story. If a narrator is telling the story, the story is in third person. If one of the characters is telling the story as himself or herself, the story is in first person. A third person narrator refers to characters in a story by the words "he," "she," "it," "they," "them," and the characters' names. Third person is the most common point of view in picture books, children's literature, and literature in general. In third person omniscient point of view, the reader finds out the thoughts of several characters. In third person limited, the reader finds out the thoughts of only one character.

A first person narrator refers to himself, herself, or itself as "I." The reader only knows the thoughts of that character and sees things the way that character sees them. Rarely used, especially in children's literature, is the second person point of view. The narrator refers to "you," as if the action is happening to the reader. A book using this point of view is *If You Take A Mouse to School* by Laura Numeroff.

Introduce point of view to your students. Read one or more of the books listed at the end of this chapter marked "POV," or choose your own favorites. Help students identify point of view. Ask them if the story is in first person or third person. Ask whose point of view is represented in the story. Even in third person, the character we are "with" on a particular page of the story is the point of view character. The reader sees what happens to that character and none of the others.

When students have a grasp of point of view, they can practice with partners. Have them choose books with obvious points of view and complete the Point of View—Who is Telling the Story? template, (Figure 1.1) They may work individually or with a partner.

FIGURE 1.1

Point of View—Who is Telling the Story?

Name(s) _____ Date _____

Choose five picture books. Read them and complete the chart below. Decide the point of view. Put an "X" in the appropriate column to indicate which person's point of view. Write the names of the main characters, circling the name of the point of view character.

BOOK TITLE	MAIN CHARACTERS	POINT OF VIEW		
		1st Person	2nd Person	3rd Person

FIGURE 1.2 Point of View Sample Rubric

OBJECTIVES	UNSATISFACTORY	SATISFACTORY	EXCELLENT	EARNED POINTS
Students will indicate understanding of definitions of point of view, 1st person, 2nd person, and 3rd person by oral participation in class.	**0-3 points** Student incorrectly defines point of view.	**4-7 points** Student correctly defines point of view.	**8-10 points** Student correctly identifies point of view, and 1st person, 2nd person, and 3rd person.	
Student will correctly define point of view, 1st person, 2nd person, 3rd person. Students will identify point of view and point of view character in 5 picture books and complete Point of View Template.	**0-3 points** Incorrectly identifies point of view and does not complete Point of View Template.	**4-7 points** Student correctly identifies either point of view or point of view character in 5 picture books and completes Point of View Template.	**8-10 points** Student correctly identifies either point of view and point of view character in 5 picture books and completes Point of View Template with 0-2 errors.	

20 possible points

Practicing Point of View

NCTE 1, 3, 4, 5, 6, 11, 12 Have each student choose a picture book. (It can be one from (Figure 1.1) Students will imagine that another character in the book is telling the story. Students will rewrite the story from that character's point of view. Then they will read their stories aloud to the class. Discuss the differences between the students' stories and the originals.

FIGURE 1.3 Presenting Point of View Sample Rubric

OBJECTIVES	UNSATISFACTORY	SATISFACTORY	EXCELLENT	EARNED POINTS
Students will write picture book story choosing a different point of view character.	**0-3 points** Student writes inconsistent point of view character.	**4-7 points** Student writes consistent point of view character.	**8-10 points** Student writes consistent point of view charachter and develops character to fit the story.	
Student will read their stories aloud and orally compare and contrast them with the original.	**0-3 points** Student does not read aloud. Student does not offer oral comparison or contrast with original.	**4-7 points** Student reads aloud and offers some oral comparison or contrast with the original.	**8-10 points** Student reads aloud and offers oral comparison or contrast with the original.	
20 possible points				

Variation

Have the class work with the same picture book, but have them each write from a different character's point of view. Upon completion, you will have as many versions of the story as there are characters or students. Have students read their stories aloud to the class. You may lead a critical discussion asking questions such as, "Did the author stay with the same point of view?" "Did the author include only those things the point of view character would see or know?" You may also have a class vote on which point of view they liked best and why.

Develop a classroom "Compare and Contrast" chart on which students can write items from their stories that are similar to the book and those that are different.

From First to Third

NCTE 1, 3, 4, 5, 6, 11, 12 Have each student choose a first person picture book and rewrite the story in third person. When students are finished, they should share with a partner or in a small group. They will discuss any difficulties they had in changing the story. Have them decide which point of view works best for the story and why.

FIGURE 1.4 From First to Third Sample Rubric

OBJECTIVES	UNSATISFACTORY	SATISFACTORY	EXCELLENT	EARNED POINTS
Students will read picture book written in first person and rewrite the story in third person.	**0-3 points** Student does not write consistent third person.	**4-7 points** Student writes consistent third person.	**8-10 points** Student writes consistent third person and adapts story to work well with changed point of view.	
Students will read their stories aloud in small groups and discuss their writing processes. Students will determine which point of view best suits the story and why.	**0-3 points** Student does not read aloud. Student does not participate in discussion or offer opinion.	**4-7 points** Student reads aloud and offers some discussion participation or opinion.	**8-10 points** Student reads aloud and offers discussion participation and opinion.	
20 possible points				

From Third to First

NCTE 1, 3, 4, 5, 6, 11, 12 Have each student choose a third person picture book and rewrite the story in first person. When students are finished, they should share with a partner or in a small group. They will discuss any difficulties they had in changing the story. Have them decide which point of view works best for the story and why.

In the Meantime

NCTE 1, 3, 4, 5, 6, 12 Define scene as an episode or section of a story. Read a picture book aloud, asking students to identify scenes. Questions to help them are, "When does something else start happening?" "When does the action shift?" *Curious George* by H.A. Rey begins with a scene in the jungle. The next scene is on the ship, followed by George arriving at the man's house. When you have identified the scenes, ask students to consider what is happening that readers are not shown. For example, when Curious George gets to the man's house, he eats, smokes, and goes to bed. Because readers see most of the story from George's point of view, they are not told about the man, but it is his house. Where is he, and what is he doing?

Have each student choose a picture book and write the scenes that are not there because of point of view limitations. What is happening to the other characters in the meantime? Write that scene.

A Reliable Source

NCTE 1, 3, 4, 5, 6, 11, 12 Introduce this activity by discussing with students how they know whom to trust and whose word to believe. Then explain that they should be as cautious about the point of view character in stories. Readers find out only what the point of view character wants them to find out. The point of view character may be interpreting things inaccurately. Read aloud any version of *Henny Penny* (Paul Galdone's is popular) and discuss the hen's interpretation of events to demonstrate the point.

Have each student choose one picture book written in third person and one written in first person. For each book have the student complete the Reliable Source template (Figure 1.5)

Extensions

- If the point of view character is reliable, rewrite the story so that the point of view character is not reliable in at least one way.

- If the point of view character is not reliable, rewrite the story so that the point of view character is reliable in at least one way.

Main Character's Thoughts

NCTE 1, 3, 4, 5, 6, 11, 12 Readers learn about a character by his or her thoughts, by physical description, and by dialogue between the main character and other characters. This lesson helps students interpret characters' thoughts as they apply to character traits. Practice together as a class using a picture book, such as *The Hard-Times Jar* by Ethel Footman Smothers. For example, on the first page, Emma thinks she needs her paper and pencil and does not want Mama to hide them. What character traits does that show? Appropriate words could include "creative," "afraid," "worried," or others. Continue identifying the character's thoughts and traits through the story. When you have finished, discuss the overall character based on the traits you have identified.

FIGURE 1.5 — A Reliable Source

Name(s) _____ Date _____

A reliable source is one that tells the truth, one that you can believe. Complete the chart below and then answer the question at the bottom.

Book Title _____ Point of View_____

In each box, write the character's name and what you know about the character. Include how well each character gets along with the point of view character.

Point of View Character	Other Main Character	Other Main Character	Other Main Character

Write your answers to the questions below. Be prepared to defend your opinions to the class.

Based on what you know from the book, is the point of view character reliable?

      Circle one: Yes   No

Is the point of view character telling the truth about the other characters?

      Circle one: Yes   No

Why do you think the character is or is not reliable?

Choose picture books that include characters' thoughts and distribute to students. Students may work individually or with partners, finding places in the story with characters' thoughts. Have them complete the Main Character's Thoughts template (Figure 1.6).

Extensions

- Change the word "Thoughts" to "Actions" in the Main Character's Thoughts template (Figure 1.6). Copy and distribute. Have students look at the same picture book they did for the Main Character's Thoughts activity. This time, they will focus on what the main character does. Students will complete the template based only on the character's actions. Then they will compare the words they circled for "thoughts" with the words they circled for "actions." Ask if this character is consistent. Is the character the same personality in thoughts and actions?

- If a character is inconsistent, students can rewrite the story so that thoughts and actions are consistent. They can share their stories with the class or in small groups and discuss how the story changed.

- Change the title of the Main Character's Thought template (Figure 1.6) to "About Me." This time, have students circle words that describe themselves. They may ask a friend if they are not sure. They will compare their circled words with the words they circled for the picture book character. Ask them how they are like the character and how they are different. Have them think about what they would do in the story if they were the main character. What would they think? How would they solve the problem or overcome the obstacle presented? Students will write the story with themselves as the main character, changing the story line to be consistent with their own traits. Share finished stories in small groups or with the entire class.

Dialogue

Dialogue, how characters talk, reveals a lot about them, just as listening to real people talk reveals a lot about them. Dialogue can tell readers about the speaker, the character being spoken to, and the character being spoken about.

Dialogue usually has special punctuation and formatting rules that set it apart from other writing. It moves the story forward quickly and is faster to read than long passages of narration. The reader's eye is drawn to dialogue because it is surrounded by white space on the page.

Read aloud a picture book with dialogue, such as *Mice Twice* by Joseph Low, and discuss with students the introductory material about dialogue. Help them discover dialogue's punctuation and formatting by asking them to look for patterns in the book's dialogue.

Getting to Know Characters Through Dialogue

NCTE 1, 3, 4, 5, 6, 11, 12 Students can learn more about character by using a picture book to complete Getting to Know Characters Through Dialogue I and II templates (Figure 1.7 and Figure 1.8). Students may work individually or in pairs.

FIGURE 1.6 — Main Character's Thoughts

Name(s) _____ Date _____

Book Title _____

Main Character _____

Below is a list of description words. Based only on the main character's thoughts, which of these describe the main character? Circle as many that apply.

Sane	Calm	Honest	Quiet	Popular	Envious
Smart	Agitated	Criminal	Good-looking	Geeky	Fearful
Slow	Nervous	Active	Homely	Rude	Confident
Kind	Mean	Lazy	Graceful	Well-mannered	Shy
Happy	Friendly	Messy	Clumsy	Forgiving	Stylish
Sad	Withdrawn	Tidy	Rich	Vengeful	Strong
Insane	Smart	Noisy	Poor	Content	Weak

If you think of other words, write them here _____

_____

Do the main character's thoughts agree with the action in the story? Why or why not?

_____

_____

_____

_____

_____

FIGURE 1.7 # Getting to Know Characters Through Dialogue I

Name(s) _____   Date _____

Book Title _____

Main Character _____

Directions: Copy your character's dialogue from the book into the first column. Include proper punctuation. In the second column, write what that segment of dialogue reveals about the character.

WHAT THE CHARACTER SAYS	WHAT THIS TELLS ABOUT THE CHARACTER

FIGURE 1.8

Getting to Know Characters Through Dialogue II

Name(s) _____   Date _____

Book Title _____

Main Character _____

What Other Characters Say About the Main Character

Directions: Use the same picture book that you used to complete Getting to Know Characters Through Dialogue Template I. In the first column, write the name of the character who is speaking about the main character. In the second column, copy from the book what the other characters say *about* the main character. Include proper punctuation. In the third column, write what that segment of dialogue reveals about the character.

CHARACTER NAME	WHAT CHARACTER SAID ABOUT MAIN CHARACTER	WHAT YOU LEARNED ABOUT MAIN CHARACTER

Giving Voice

NCTE 1, 3, 4, 5, 6, 11, 12 Provide a selection of picture books in which the main character does not talk, such as *Curious George* by H.A. Rey or wordless picture books. Ask students to write dialogue for the main character, individually or with partners. As they write, they should write down the corresponding book page number. Have students present their dialogue with the book when everyone is ready.

Hello? Is It You?

NCTE 1, 3, 4, 5, 6, 11, 12 Ask students if they have ever eavesdropped on one side of a conversation. For example, they may have overheard one side of a parent's telephone conversation. Explain that eavesdropping is considered rude, but professional writers do pay attention to the spoken words around them. Ask students how much they could understand of the conversation. Ask if they have ever guessed incorrectly about what was said.

Use *Ring! Yo?* by Chris Raschka, which presents only one side of a telephone conversation. Or choose a picture book with dialogue, and put an opaque piece of paper over one character's speech throughout the book. Read one character's speech, showing the book's page, as pictures give contextual clues. Pause and have students write what they think is the other character's reply. When you have read the story through and students have written their responses, read the story again. This time, read one character's speech and have a volunteer read his or her response. Allow time for at least three volunteers. Ask if other students had similar or different responses. Then reveal the full dialogue as it appears in the book. Discuss how the students' versions of the story changed from the original.

Standard English or Slang?

NCTE 1, 3, 4, 5, 6, 11, 12 Since dialogue reflects the way real people talk, some dialogue may be written in slang or non-standard English. Define slang and non-standard English and give examples. Ask students to list some common slang terms, such as *awesome, bad*, and *cool*. Explain that non-standard English includes ungrammatical usage, such as *he don't* and *ain't*. The library media specialist can introduce standard and slang dictionaries, and direct students to dictionary Web sites as references. *Scholastic Children's Dictionary*, NY: Scholastic, 2002, and *Scholastic Dictionary of Idioms*, NY: Scholastic, 1998, are two print sources.

Ask students if people in their families have their own special sayings. Ask if they know people who use interesting expressions (that are appropriate for the classroom). Read a picture book containing dialogue with slang or non-standard English, such as *Saving Sweetness* by Diane Stanley, and have students raise their hands when they hear such dialogue. When you have completed the story, ask students how they would change the non-standard English into standard English. Then ask, which fits the character better?

Have students choose a picture book with dialogue written in non-standard English. They will rewrite the story, changing the dialogue into standard English. When everyone is ready, have volunteers read both versions to the class. Discuss which version is truest to the character.

Extension

Choose a picture book with dialogue written in standard English. Ask students to rewrite the story, changing the dialogue of one character into non-standard English. Students may use school-appropriate slang, idioms, colloquialisms, and dialect. Have them try to stay true to the character. Demonstrate by reading aloud a segment of a well-known character's dialogue. Ask students how to use slang to say the same thing. Then ask if the character would talk like that. Keep refining until you have dialogue in less standard English, but is representative of something the character would really say. When all have completed their slang dialogue, volunteers will read both versions to the class. Discuss which version is truest to the character.

What Can I Say?

NCTE 1, 2, 3, 4, 5, 6, 9, 11, 12

After some practice with dialogue, have a selection of picture books available. Allow students time to read several. Then copy and distribute the What Can I Say? template (Figure 1.9). Students will work individually or with partners to complete the template. When everyone is ready, have students read their stories aloud to the class. If students work with partners, they can each take a role in reading the dialogue, as if it were a play. You may like to have the class guess the characters and the books.

Acrostic Characters

NCTE 1, 2, 3, 4, 5, 6, 9, 11, 12

Have each student choose a favorite picture book character. Then ask them to write an acrostic poem using the character's name and adjectives about the character. Write one together as a class first for practice.

For example:

Sophie, from *When Sophie Gets Angry—Really, Really Angry* by Molly Bang
Stubborn
Ornery
Pouting
Hiding
Impish
Excited

Students may write their poems on paper or on the computer using a word processing program. Students may decorate their poems with general art supplies or graphics software. Display them in the classroom when they are completed.

FIGURE 1.9 # What Can I Say?

Name(s) _____ Date _____

What if (character name) _____ from (picture book title)

_____ met (different character name) _____

from (different picture book title) _____?

What would they say to each other?

Write their dialogue below. Use proper format and punctuation. Try to reveal who the
characters are by what they say.

_____

_____

_____

_____

_____

_____

_____

_____

_____

_____

_____

_____

_____

_____

_____

_____

Physical Description

NCTE 1, 2, 3, 11, 12 Readers learn about characters by the way the writer describes characters physically. Picture books do not usually have much physical description in the text. The illustrator makes the character's physical nature come alive.

Have students work in pairs. Each pair should choose several picture books with strong character and complete The Way You Look template (Figure 1.10). When everyone has completed the template, discuss the results as a class. If more than one pair used the same book, did they get similar results?

Extensions

Have students draw a picture of their characters to accompany their character sketches and display the results.

My, How You've Grown

NCTE 1, 2, 3, 4, 5, 6, 11, 12 A well-drawn character should show some growth or change during the course of the story. The character will face some problem or conflict that is resolved somehow, which forces the character to learn something.

Choose a picture book with strong characters. Read it aloud, and then ask students what the character has learned or how the character's personality has changed. Go through the book again, page by page, to see where and why the changes occurred.

Then have students do their own study of character development by choosing a picture book with strong character and completing the My, How You've Grown template (Figure 1.11). Students will share results with the class when everyone has completed the template.

Then ask students to think of a time they faced a problem and grew from the experience. Have them write about it. They can think of themselves as a "character," and use the My, How You've Grown template (Figure 1.11) as a planning tool, if they like. Volunteers will share with the class, or partners will share with each other.

It's Problematic

NCTE 1, 2, 3, 4, 5, 6, 11, 12 In a good story, all main characters must have a goal or face a problem of some sort. Choose a picture book with strong characters and read it aloud to the class. Then have the class identify the main character's problem or goal and the steps the character takes to solve the problem or reach the goal.

Next, students will choose a picture book with strong characters. They will identify the main character's problems or goals. Then they will write their analysis in the form of an advice column by completing the Dear Advisor template (Figure 1.12). (If students are not familiar with the advice column format, provide examples from newspapers or magazines to read first.) Have volunteers share their results with the class.

FIGURE 1.10 # The Way You Look

Name(s) _____ Date _____

Read several picture books and look for *written* physical descriptions of the characters.
A physical description includes a character's body, movements, gestures, facial expressions,
mannerisms, clothing, and name. Complete the columns below.

TITLE OF BOOK	NAME OF CHARACTER	PHYSICAL DESCRIPTION	DOES DESCRIPTION FIT PERSONALITY?

FIGURE 1.11 # My, How You've Grown

Name(s) _____   Date _____

Title of Book _____

Main Character _____

Start at the bottom of the growth chart and work your way up. Use both story text and pictures to describe character growth.

Describe character change at end: _____

_____

Evidence from story: _____

_____

_____

Describe character change as character faces problem: _____

_____

Evidence from story: _____

_____

_____

What was character like at the beginning of the story? _____

_____

_____

Evidence from story: _____

_____

_____

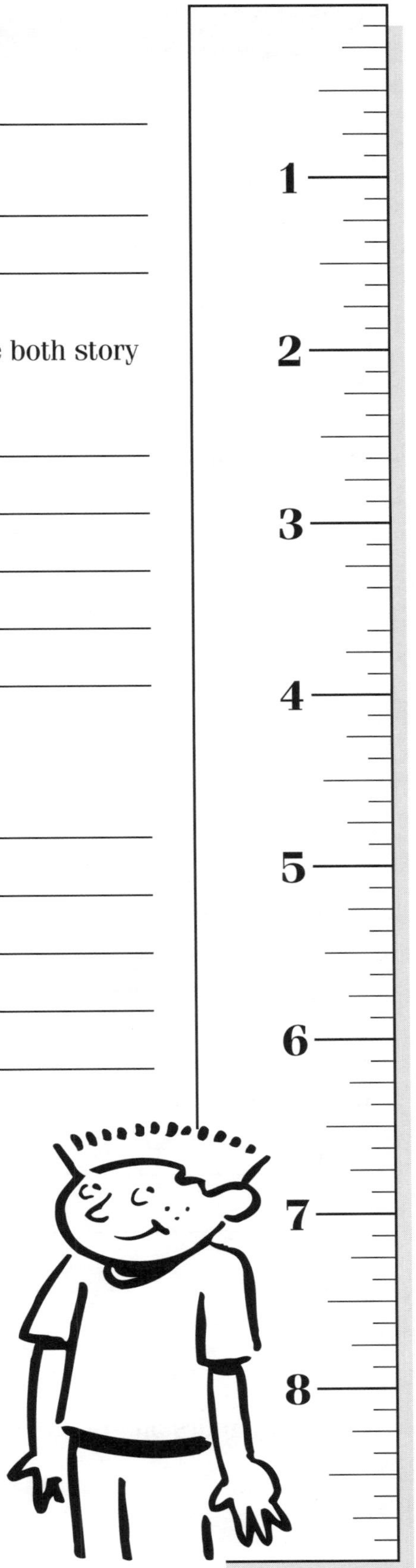

1
2
3
4
5
6
7
8

FIGURE 1.12 Dear Advisor

Name(s) _____ Date _____

Title of Book _____

Main Character _____

Imagine that you are the main character. Write to an advice columnist about your goal or problem.

••

Dear Advisor,

_____

_____

_____

_____

_____.

Signed,

_____ (Character name)

••

Now imagine that you are the advice columnist. Write your advice to the character, based on what happens in the story.

Dear _____, (Character name)

_____

_____

_____

Very Truly Yours and Good Luck,

The Advisor

Variations

- Have students complete the advice activity as themselves, giving their own advice rather than relying on what happened in the book.

- Students will write the main character's parts and then pass them to a classmate who will write the advice part.

- Students will rewrite the story so that the main character uses the advice he or she has been given in the advice column. They will read their versions aloud and discuss as a class how the advice created new problems.

Create a Character

NCTE 1, 2, 3, 4, 5, 6, 11, 12 In creating a character, the author must know more about the character than what appears in the story. Have students complete the Create a Character template (Figure 1.13). Then ask them to write a character sketch or story based on their template. Have them share results aloud with the class.

Extension

Authors who create characters often find pictures in magazines or catalogs to give them a visual to keep in mind. British children's author Pamela Cleaver recommends this practice in *Writing a Children's Book* (51). Newbery Award winner, Ellen Raskin, used clipped pictures to create characters for *The Westing Game* (Dutton, 2003). See <http://www.soemadison.wisc.edu/ccbc/wisauth/raskin/notes.htm> for more about Raskin and her book.) Have students draw pictures of their character or find pictures in magazines or catalogs that depict their characters. They may also use computer graphics software or Internet resources, keeping copyright restrictions in mind. Have students show the results to the class. Ask students, "What does your picture show about your character?"

Variations

- Have students complete a Create a Character template (Figure 1.13) based on the main character of one of the picture books they have read or heard. Have students share results in small groups, with the other students guessing to which character each template refers.

- Have students exchange Create a Character templates (Figure1.13) with a partner, based on picture books they have read or heard. Students will write a character sketch or short story based on the template they receive. Partners will share their sketches or stories with each other. Then have them reveal the character upon which the template was based. Ask if the characters they created are anything like the original picture book character. Then ask why or why not.

FIGURE 1.13 # Create a Character

Name(s) _____   Date _____

To create a believable character, you must know much more about the character than appears in a story. You must know the character like you know your best friend. Imagine an original character and complete the following chart.

Full Character Name _____

Nickname? _____

Circle one: Male   Female   Animal (which one)_____

Other (specify)_____

Age_____   Grade (if in school) _____

Full Address _____

Family _____

Type of Dwelling _____

Favorites:

    Color_____   Season_____

    TV Show _____   Movie _____

    Book_____   Clothes_____

    Music_____   School Subject_____

    Sport_____   Pastime_____

    Friend_____

Looks Like _____

_____

Values (What is most important to your character?) _____

_____

Now think about this character. Write a character sketch or short story about the character you've created.

Wanted!

NCTE 1, 2, 3, 4, 5, 6, 11, 12 Choose picture books with strong characters that have an obvious villain (folktales and fairy tales are especially good for this). Discuss with the class the type of information usually found on wanted posters. Bring in samples, if possible, or show a clip from TV's "America's Most Wanted," taking care to comply with federal copyright law. Usually included in descriptions are scars or identifying physical characteristics, name, alias, where last seen, clothing, why the person is wanted, and how dangerous the person is.

Collaborate with the art teacher or technology teacher. Provide general art supplies or computers with graphics software. Have students choose a villain from among those in picture books they have read. Students will make wanted posters of the villains, drawing pictures and adding information generated in discussion. Post them in the classroom when everyone is finished.

Diamente Foils

NCTE 2, 3, 4, 5, 6, 11, 12 Authors often use two characters with opposite character traits to play off each other, emphasize the theme, and heighten conflict. In literature, these characters are called "foils." Choose picture books that have characters acting as foils, such as the main characters in *Hunter's Best Friend at School* by Laura Malone Elliott. Read one as an example and ask students to compare the characters. Then explain the diamente poetic form, which takes its name from its diamond shape. It is seven lines long, centered on the page. The traditional form contains antonyms in lines 1 and 7 and descriptive words about those nouns. The form is:

Line 1   One noun, an antonym or contrast to Line 7, in this case, the name of a character
Line 2   Two adjectives that describe Line 1
Line 3   Three gerunds (verbs with –ing endings) that relate to Line 1
Line 4   Four nouns, the first two relate to Line 1, the second two relate to Line 7
Line 5   Three gerunds that relate to Line 7
Line 6   Two adjectives that describe Line 7
Line 7   One noun, an antonym or contrast to Line 1, in this case, the name of the opposing character

Write a class diamente poem using the names of the picture book characters you discussed as foils as lines 1 and 7. An example using the characters in *Hunter's Best Friend at School* follows:

Hunter
Thoughtful, ethical
Following, caring, helping
Scholar, friend, friend, clown
Attention-seeking, fun-loving, leading,
Mischievous, Troublesome
Stripe

FIGURE 1.14 **Character Diamente**

Name(s) _____

Book Title _____

_____

(character name)

_____, _____

(two adjectives describing Line 1)

_____ing, _____ing, _____ing

(three verbs relating to Line 1)

_____, _____, _____, _____

(two nouns relating to Line 1, two nouns relating to Line 7)

_____ing, _____ing, _____ing

(three verbs relating to Line 7)

_____, _____

(two adjectives describing Line 7)

_____

(name of opposite character)

Students can work with partners or in small groups. Each group will choose one of the selected books, decide which characters are foils, and consider the characters' traits. Distribute the Character Diamente template (Figure 1.14), and have each group write a diamente beginning with one character's name and ending with the foil character's name. When the groups are finished, they will share their poems aloud in class and post them for display.

Greetings!

| NCTE 2, 3, 4, 5, 6, 11, 12 | Collaborate with the art teacher or technology teacher. Provide general art supplies or computers with graphics software. Have students use traditional art supplies or computer graphics software to make a greeting card to send to a story's main character. The card can be seasonal, or it can relate to something that happens in the story.

Variation

- Students will make a greeting card from one character in the story to another.

- Students will send a postcard or short letter to the story's main character.

Qualified

| NCTE 2, 3, 4, 5, 6, 11, 12 | This activity is appropriate for the classroom or the library, led by the teacher, the library media specialist, or both. Expose students to the broad world of work by discussing jobs with which they are familiar. The library media specialist can expand students' knowledge by showing them career books and the U.S. Government publication, *Occupational Outlook Handbook*, available in print or online at <http://purl.access.gpo.gov/GPO/LPS4235>. Tell students that people looking for jobs are often required to furnish the potential employer with a resume. A resume shows a person's work and educational experience to the person's best advantage. The library media specialist can find books and Web sites with sample resumes. One Web site is <www.monster.com>.

When students are familiar with resume format and content, have them work individually or with a partner to choose a picture book main character and consider for which type of job he or she would apply. Then students will write resumes for their characters.

When everyone has completed the resumes, create panels of three or four students. Circulate the resumes among the panels. The panels should answer the questions "Would you hire this character?" "Why or why not?"

Extension

Have students write resumes for themselves. Resumes may be for paying or non-paying jobs they currently hold or for a job they would like to have in the future.

Going Commercial

NCTE 2, 3, 4, 5, 6, 11, 12 Tell students that the next set of action figures for a restaurant kids' meal promotion will be picture book characters. Their job is to design and describe the action figures and write the ad. Have students work with partners or in small groups. They may choose their own character or set of characters from a picture book. They may draw or make a model of the product, if they like. When the groups have completed the assignment, they should present their ad campaign to the rest of the class.

A Day in the Life

NCTE 2, 3, 4, 5, 6, 11, 12 Explain to students that many people and most writers keep a journal or diary. A journal is a safe place to write thoughts and express emotions and opinions. A diary is an account of what happened on a particular day. Show examples, if possible. (*Diary of a Worm* by Doreen Cronin is one.) Have students choose a picture book main character and write a journal or diary entry that the main character might write, or write "A Day in the Life of...." Volunteers may share their entries aloud with the class.

Welcome, Guest

NCTE 2, 3, 4, 5, 6, 11, 12 After students have become familiar with a variety of picture book characters, have them each choose one to invite to class for a visit. Distribute You're Invited templates (Figure 1.15). When students have completed their templates, display them in the classroom.

Extensions

- Some schools and costume shops have picture book character costumes available. Or have creative adult volunteers make a costume. Have a character accept an invitation and actually visit the classroom. The visiting character could be the library media specialist, giving a talk about the author who created his or her character.

- Have students use general art supplies or computer graphics software to create posters welcoming their character to your class.

Talk Show Talk

NCTE 1, 2, 3, 4, 5, 6, 8, 11, 12 After students have heard or read a variety of picture books, have them develop a TV talk show with characters from different books as guests. Have students work in groups, writing a script for their character's segment. Each group will write a script containing the talk show host's questions and the character's answers. Assign student actors or have them volunteer for certain parts (in the case of a tie, an audition may be necessary). Be as simple or as elaborate as you like. Use costumes, masks, or hats to distinguish characters. The teacher's desk can serve as the talk show host's desk, with one chair for each guest. Students who are not actors are the studio audience. Rehearse a time or two, and then videotape the show. Play it back so actors can see themselves.

FIGURE 1.15 **You're Invited**

Name(s) _____

Book Title _____

Character _____

You're Invited!

Who: _____ (your name) of _____ (your class)

invites you to

What: a classroom visit

When: _____ (day, date, and time)

Where: _____ (your school name and address)

Why: We would like to meet you because _____

_____.

_____

You would like us because _____

_____.

_____ (school phone number)

RSVP to _____ (your teacher) at _____

Extension

Perform your talk show for other classes, parent nights, or other special events.

Get Out the Vote

NCTE 1, 2, 3, 4, 5, 6, 7, 11, 12   Learning to present a persuasive argument is an important skill. Show students examples of letters to the editor of your local newspaper, covering the letter-writer's name. Discuss how effective the letter writer is. Examine the letters to see if the writers have appealed to logic, emotions, or both. What techniques have the writers used to persuade their readers? Have they presented facts or given anecdotes?

Following the discussion, have students choose a picture book character. Ask them to imagine that the character is running for mayor of your town. Based on what the students know about their character, they will write a letter to the editor of the newspaper persuading others to elect their character. When everyone has completed their letters, have students read them aloud to the class and conduct a class vote to see which character wins.

Variation

Instead of reading their letters aloud to the class, have students type their letters into a computer word processing program. Then print the letters, distributing them to the class. After the class has read the letters, have them cast their ballots.

My Favorite Character

NCTE 1, 2, 3, 4, 5, 6, 11, 12   After students have heard or read many picture books with strong characters, ask them to review several picture books and write an essay answering the question "Who is your favorite character and why?" The essay should be at least five paragraphs long. The first paragraph should be an introduction, the last paragraph should be a conclusion, and each of the middle paragraphs (the body) should give one reason. Before students begin writing, distribute Figure 1.16 My Favorite Character Rubric or one the library media specialist or teacher has developed. When students' essays are finished, have them evaluate their own work using the rubric. Students will hand in their essays and rubrics. The teacher or library media specialist will assess the students' work using a blank copy of the same rubric.

Welcome to My World

NCTE 1, 2, 3, 4, 5, 6, 11, 12   After students have read or heard a variety of picture books, have them choose a story character. Then ask students to write what life would be like if that character moved in with them. Have them consider how their families and friends would react, how their lives at school would change, how their daily routines would change, and how their activities would be affected. Volunteers will read their results to the class, or all students will share their results in small groups.

FIGURE 1.16　My Favorite Character Rubric

Name of Student Being Assessed _____

Title of Assessor _____

OBJECTIVES	UNSATISFACTORY	SATISFACTORY	EXCELLENT	EARNED POINTS
Student will review picture book characters, choose a favorite, and think of three reasons why that character is a favorite as indicated on student's planning notes.	**1 point** Student chooses a character based on reviewing three or fewer books and has one reason why the character is a favorite.	**2 points** Student chooses a character based on reviewing five books and notes three reasons why that character is a favorite.	**3 points** Student chooses a character based on reviewing more than five books and notes three reasons why that character is a favorite.	
Student will write a five-paragraph essay explaining why that character is the favorite. Paragraph one is an introduction, paragraph five is the conclusion, paragraphs two through four are the body. The body contains one reason for each paragraph.	**15 points** Student writes four or fewer paragraphs.	**16 points** Student writes an introduction, conclusion, and three paragraphs of body explaining why the character is a favorite.	**17 points** Student writes an introduction, conclusion, and three paragraphs of body explaining why the character is a favorite. Paragraphs are well-developed with convincing reasons.	
20 possible points			**Score:**	

Assessor Comments:

Picture Books with Strong Characters

Books marked "POV" refer to those with strong point of view characters or narrators.

Ackerman, Karen. *Song and Dance Man*, New York: Knopf, Reprint ed., 1992. Grandchildren see a new side of their grandfather when he demonstrates his vaudeville songs and dances.

Agran, Rick. *Pumpkin Shivaree*, New York: Handprint, 2003. POV A pumpkin tells its life story.

Allard, Harry. *Miss Nelson Is Missing,* Boston: Houghton, Reissue ed., 1985. Students misbehave for Miss Nelson. She is replaced by an evil substitute—or is she?

Bang, Molly. *When Sophie Gets Angry—Really, Really Angry*, New York: Scholastic, 1999. When Sophie gets angry, she leaves the scene and collects herself before returning.

Bearden, Romare. *Li'l Dan the Drummer Boy*, New York: Simon, 2003. Li'l Dan follows a company of black Union soldiers and saves them from attack.

Birnbaum, Abe. *Green Eyes*, New York: Golden, Deluxe ed., 2001. POV. A white cat with green eyes tells about it's first year of life.

Briggs, Raymond. *The Snowman*, New York: Random, 1978. A boy's snowman comes to life and takes the boy flying.

Cohen, Miriam. *Will I Have a Friend?,* New York: Aladdin, Reprint ed., 1989. POV Jim worries and wonders about whether he will have a friend when he starts kindergarten.

Cronin, Doreen. *Diary of a Worm*, New York: Joanna Cotler, 2003. POV It's a worm's life, as written in funny diary entries by a young boy worm.

DeGroat, Diane. *Roses are Pink, Your Feet Really Stink,* New York: Harper, Reprint ed., 1997. Gilbert forges names on mean Valentines and gets into trouble.

De Paola, Tomie. *Nana Upstairs & Nana Downstairs*, New York: Puffin, Reissue ed., 2000. A young boy learns about death in loving his grandmother and ill great-grandmother.

_____. *Strega Nona,* New York: Aladdin, 1979. Strega Nona, an Italian witch, has a magic pasta pot. When Big Anthony, Strega Nona's helper, learns the spell, he cannot stop it!

Dorros, Arthur. *Abuela*, Glenview, IL: Foresman, Reprint ed., 1997. A young girl rides on a bus with her grandmother and imagines that they are flying over New York City.

Ehlert, Lois. *Top Cat,* San Diego, CA: Voyager, Reprint ed., 2001. POV The top cat of the house is jealous of the new kitten, but shares its survival secrets.

Elliott, Laura Malone. *Hunter's Best Friend at School,* New York: Harper, 2002. Hunter and Stripe are best friends. But when Hunter follows Stripe's lead, he gets into trouble at school. Can he behave and remain friends with Stripe?

Falconer, Ian. *Olivia,* New York: Atheneum, 2000. Olivia, a young pig, throws her energy into everything she does.

Fisher, Valerie. *My Big Sister*, New York: Atheneum, 2003. POV A baby tells about her big sister, from baby's point of view in story and photos.

Fleming, Denise. *Buster*, New York: Holt, 2003. POV Buster, the dog, learns courage when he loses his fear of the cat that joins his household.

Galdone, Paul. *Henny Penny,* New York: Clarion, 1979. POV One version of this classic tale. The hen alarms everyone with her cry, "The sky is falling!" But is it?

_____. *The Magic Porridge Pot,* New York: Clarion, 1979. POV The magic porridge pot feeds the little girl, but does not work as well for her mother.

Gantos, Jack. *Rotten Ralph's Rotten Romance,* Boston: Houghton, 1997. Rotten Ralph, a very bad cat, tries to ruin Valentine's Day, only to have his plan backfire on him.

Goble, Paul. *The Girl Who Loved Wild Horses,* Glenview, IL: Foresman, Reissue ed., 1993. A retold Native American tale. A girl loves her people, but loves the wild horses more. Her village releases her to them, and they run away together.

Graham, Bob. *Crusher is Coming,* South Melbourne, Australia: Lothian, 2000. POV Peter does not want to look like a wimp when his football-player friend, Crusher, comes to visit. Peter is surprised to discover Crusher's good manners and choice of play.

Graves, Keith. *Frank Was a Monster Who Wanted to Dance,* San Francisco: Chronicle, 1999. Frank loves to dance—until it undoes him.

Greenfield, Eloise. *Me and Neesie,* New York: Harper, 2004. POV. Janell's invisible friend, Neesie, interferes with Aunt Bea's visit.

_____. *She Come Bringing Me That Little Baby Girl,* New York: Harper, Reprint ed., 1993. Learning how important a big brother can be takes away Kevin's jealousy and disappointment at the arrival of a baby sister.

Havill, Juanita. *Jamaica Tag-Along,* Boston: Houghton, Reprint ed., 1989. POV Hurt because her big brother will not let her play with him, she allows younger children to play tag with her.

Henkes, Kevin. *Chrysanthemum,* New York: Harper, 1996. When Chrysanthemum starts school, everyone makes fun of her beloved name.

_____. *Julius, the Baby of the World,* New York: Morrow, 1990. Lilly finds her new baby brother disgusting, until she defends him against her cousin.

_____. *Lilly's Purple Plastic Purse,* New York: Greenwillow, 1996. Lilly is so proud of her purse that she disobeys her beloved teacher and plays with it during class. He takes her purse and puts a kind note inside, but Lilly writes her own mean note to the teacher. Lilly learns how to apologize and reconcile.

_____. *Owen,* New York: Greenwillow, 1993. Owen and his parents find a way for him to give up his blanket and keep it at the same time.

Hoban, Lillian. *Arthur's Great Big Valentine,* New York: Harper, Reprint ed., 1991. Arthur and his best friend are not getting along, but make up using special Valentines.

Hoban, Russell. *Bread and Jam for Frances,* New York: Harper, Reprint ed., 1993. Frances loves jam and eats it on bread every day until she has too much.

Hoffman, Mary. *Amazing Grace.* Glenview, IL: Foresman, 1991. In spite of race and gender, Grace proves she can be Peter Pan.

Hort, Lenny. *How Many Stars in the Sky?,* New York: Harper, Reprint ed., 1997. POV Mama is away and her son and husband cannot sleep. Father and son drive into the country, lie on their backs, and count the stars.

Keats, Ezra Jack. *Whistle for Willie,* New York: Viking, 1964. POV Peter tries to learn to whistle for his dog, Willie. After many unsuccessful tries, finally something comes out.

Kraus, Robert. *Leo the Late Bloomer,* New York: Harper, Reissue ed., 1994. Leo, the lion cub, is not keeping up with his friends in his learning. His parents watch and encourage him until he blooms.

Krensky, Stephen. *My Teacher's Secret Life,* New York: Aladdin, 1999. POV A child discovers that teachers do not really live at school.

Lester, Helen. *Hooway for Wodney Wat,* Boston: Houghton, 1999. Wodney Wat, much maligned for his speech impediment, uses his handicap to eliminate a bully from his class.

_____. *Tacky the Penguin,* Boston: Houghton Mifflin, 1988. Tacky does not behave like a typical penguin, but his oddities help thwart hunters and save his friends.

Lionni, Leo. *Alexander and the Wind-Up Mouse,* New York: Dragonfly, Reissue ed., 1974. Alexander is lonely and threatened. He befriends Willy, the wind-up mouse, and wants to be like him. Then he learns that Willy is in the garbage. Alexander finds a magical way for them to them to stay together.

_____. *Frederick,* New York: Knopf, Reissue ed., 1967. Frederick, the mouse, does not toil like his brothers, but he shares his special talents to help them all last through winter.

Lobel, Arnold. *Frog and Toad Are Friends,* New York: Harper, 1970. Frog and Toad show what being best friends is all about in this book of five stories.

_____. *Frog and Toad Together,* New York: Harper, 1972. Frog and Toad demonstrate the power of friendship.

_____. *On Market Street,* New York: Greenwillow, 1981. POV A rhyming alphabet story, the main character buys gifts from A to Z on Market Street.

London, Jonathan. *Froggy Plays Soccer,* New York: Puffin, 2001. Froggy's team makes the city soccer play-offs, but almost loses the game because of Froggy's mistake.

Low, Joseph. *Mice Twice,* New York: Aladdin, Reprint ed., 1986. Cat invites Mouse and Dog for dinner, leading to other inappropriate invitations and motives.

Marshall, James. *George and Martha,* Boston: Houghton, 1972. The ups and downs of friendship as shown by two hippos.

_____. *Yummers!,* Boston: Houghton, 1973. POV Emily Pig tries to follow Eugene Turtle's advice about walking to lose weight, but she keeps walking into temptation.

Mayer, Mercer. *A Boy, a Dog, and a Frog,* New York: Dial, 2003. POV Pictures depict the boy's difficulty in capturing a frog.

_____. *One Frog Too Many,* New York: Dial, 2003. POV One pet frog is jealous of the new pet frog.

McAllister, Angela. *The Little Blue Rabbit,* New York: Bloomsbury, 2003. POV The little blue toy rabbit is left behind and misses his boy. The other toys comfort him until his boy returns.

McCarty, Peter. *Hondo and Fabian,* New York: Holt, 2002. Hondo, the dog, and Fabian, the cat, spend their days very differently, but satisfactorily.

McKee, David. *Elmer,* New York: Harper, 1989. Elmer, the elephant, is a patchwork of colors and patterns, not at all like his elephant friends. He learns to appreciate his individuality.

McKissack, Patricia. *Flossie and the Fox,* New York: Dutton, 1986. Flossie refuses to be afraid of the fox unless he can prove who he is. In the end, she out-foxes the fox.

McPhail, David. *Pig Pig Grows Up,* Topeka, KS: Bt Bound, 1999. Pig Pig wants to remain a baby and refuses to grow up until an emergency forces him to mature.

Mora, Pat. *Tomas and the Library Lady,* New York: Knopf, 1997. Tomas, the child of migrant workers, finds the world at his fingertips at the public library.

Numeroff, Laura. *If You Take a Mouse to School*, New York: HarperCollins, 2002. If you take a mouse to school, all kinds of things will happen!

Nye, Naomi Shihab. *Baby Radar*, New York: Greenwillow, 2003. POV A toddler's eye view of the world from a stroller.

Potter, Beatrix. *The Tale of Peter Rabbit*, New York: Warner, 2002. Peter disobeys and enters Farmer McGregor's garden. He narrowly escapes and returns home to his mother's care.

Prigger, Mary Skillings. *Aunt Minnie McGranahan*, New York: Clarion, 1999. Minnie, a spinster, takes in nine orphaned nieces and nephews.

Rahaman, Vashanti. *Read for Me, Mama,* Honesdale, PA: Boyds Mills, 1997. A boy who loves to read helps his mother overcome illiteracy.

Raschka, Chris. *Ring! Yo?*, New York: DK, 2000. POV The reader gets one side of a telephone conversation in which two friends argue and make up.

Rathmann, Peggy. *Officer Buckle and Gloria*, New York: Putnam, 1995. Officer Buckle's school safety speeches improve dramatically with the help of his canine partner, Gloria.

Rey, H.A. *Curious George,* Boston: Houghton, 1973. The first of the popular series, a man finds George in the jungle and brings him to the city, where his curiosity gets him into trouble.

Ringold, Faith. *Tar Beach,* New York: Dragonfly, 1996. A young girl imagines flying above her Harlem home, making everything hers.

Ryan, Pamela Muñoz. *When Marian Sang*, New York: Scholastic, 2002. True story of Marian Anderson's singing career and the obstacles she faced because of race.

Rylant, Cynthia. *Henry and Mudge*, New York: Aladdin, Reprint ed., 1996. Henry finds friendship in his childless neighborhood when his parents let him get a dog.

_____. *When I Was Young in the Mountains,* New York: Puffin, 1993. POV An autobiographical story about the pleasures of growing up in the mountains.

San Souci, Robert D. *A Weave of Words*, New York: Orchard, 1998. Retold Armenian tale. A prince learns typically unprincely skills, which gain him love and life.

Sceiszka, Jon. *The True Story of the Three Little Pigs*, New York: Kestrel, 1989. POV The wolf insists he was framed in this twist on the traditional "Three Little Pigs."

Schachner, Judith Byron. *The Grannyman*, New York: Dutton, 1999. Simon, the cat, is given a new lease on life when he is expected to raise a kitten.

_____. *Skippyjon Jones*, New York: Dutton, 2003. Skippyjon, the cat, has delusions of grandeur as he dreams of being El Skippito.

Sendak, Maurice. *Pierre*, New York: Harper, 1990, 1962. Pierre's favorite phrase "I don't care," does not serve him well in the end.

Shannon, George. *Lizard's Song*, Topeka, KS: Bt Bound, 1999. Bear tries to sing Lizard's song, but he cannot sing it as well as Lizard.

Smothers, Ethel Footman. *The Hard-Times Jar*, New York: Farrar, 2003. Emma, the daughter of a poor migrant family, is thrilled to find a library in her new classroom. She takes a book without permission and her mother helps her find a special use for the money in the hard-times jar.

Soto, Gary. *Chato's Kitchen*, New York: Putnam, 1995. Chato, the cat, cooks special food to lure the mice he is supposed to catch.

Stanley, Diane. *Saving Sweetness*, New York: Putnam, 1996. POV The sheriff, who is telling the story, tells readers how he saved the little orphan, Sweetness. The pictures show the truth.

Steig, William. *Dr. De Soto*, New York: Farrar, 1982. Dentist Dr. De Soto and his wife, both mice, want to help anyone with toothaches. They conceive an ingenious plan to outsmart one of their patients, a fox looking for an easy lunch.

Steptoe, John. *Stevie*, Topeka, KS: Bt Bound, 1999. Robert gets tired of Stevie and wants him to go away. After Stevie is gone, Robert misses him.

Stewart, Sarah. *The Gardener*, New York: Farrar, 1997. Set during the Depression, young Lydia Grace is sent from her farm home to live in the city with her uncle. She transforms the place with her gardening.

Trivizas, Eugene. *The Three Little Wolves and the Big Bad Pig*, New York: McElderry, 1993. POV A twist on the traditional "Three Little Pigs," this time the pig is after the wolves. The wolves build various types of houses and finally find a way to tame the pig.

Viorst, Judith. *I'll Fix Anthony*, Topeka, KS: Bt Bound, 1999. POV Sibling rivalry at its best, with Anthony's little brother plotting revenge.

Wells, Rosemary. *Hazel's Amazing Mother*, Topeka, KS: Bt Bound, 2001. Mom, a badger, comes to the rescue when Hazel runs into bullies, various animals, who destroy her favorite doll.

Williams, Suzanne. *Library Lil*, New York: Dial, 1997. Library Lil turns even the unlikeliest people into readers.

Williams, Vera B. *A Chair for my Mother*, New York: Greenwillow, 1982. A young daughter, grandmother, and waitress mother save money to buy a new chair after they lose their things in a fire.

Wood, Audrey. *King Bidgood's in the Bathtub*, New York: Harcourt, 1985. POV The King is in the bathtub. The members of his court plead, but he succeeds in getting them into the tub, too. The King will not come out until a young page pulls the drain plug.

Yolen, Jane. *The Musicians of Bremen*, New York: Simon, 1996. POV A retelling of the traditional tale, four animals too old to farm try to make their way as musicians, only to discover a thieves' hideout.

CHAPTER 2

Setting

Setting is defined as the location (where) and time (when) a story takes place. In some cases, the setting is the story's most important element. That particular story could not take place anywhere else, such as *Polar Express* by Chris Van Allsburg, or at any other time, such as *Arthur's Great Big Valentine* by Lillian Hoban. Some settings are so strong that they almost become characters, such as the house in *The Napping House* by Audrey Wood.

Discuss setting with students by asking what their favorite places are and why. Ask what places they like to read about. Ask what historical period, time of year, time of day, season, and weather they like best and why. Students can make a list of their favorite settings to be used later when they select books for pleasure reading. Be prepared to answer the questions yourself. These are all components of setting.

Place

Transplantation

NCTE 1, 2, 3, 5, 6, 11, 12 — Choose a picture book with a strong sense of place. Read the story aloud, showing the illustrations as you go. You may like to read a version of the Russian folktale, *Baba Yaga*, (Katya Arnold's is one), and then read *Alice Nizzy Nazzy* by Tony Johnston, for example. Ask students to compare and contrast the story. What difference did place make in the story? Then ask students to rewrite the story but set it in a different place. They will transplant the original characters and plot into a setting different from the original story. For example, if you read *When I Was Young in the Mountains* by Cynthia Rylant, have students write the story set at the sea, on the plains, or in a city. Have them read their stories aloud to the class. Ask, "How has transplanting the plot and characters into a new place changed the story from the original?"

This Special Place

NCTE 1, 2, 3, 4, 5, 6, 11, 12 Choose a picture book with a strong sense of place, such as *Weslandia* by Paul Fleischman. Read it once for the class, showing the illustrations. Or use a wordless book such as *Sector 7* by David Wiesner, showing the pictures. Then read it again and ask students to jot down what is special about the place in the book. Ask them to listen and watch for how the author and illustrator show how special the place is. Discuss their answers. Then ask them to write a description of a special place based on what they wrote. It can be the same place as the book or a different place. Volunteers will read their descriptions aloud to the class, or all students will read to each other in small groups.

Extension

Ask students to think about a place that is special to them. Have them jot down descriptors as they think. Using techniques similar to those the author used in the picture book read to the class, students will write descriptions of their special places. Have students read to each other in small groups, with listeners evaluating based on whether they understood why the places are special.

Senses Census

NCTE 1, 2, 3, 4, 5, 6, 11, 12 Good description involves as many of our five senses as possible. Choose a picture book with strong setting, such as *Owl Moon* by Jane Yolen, and read it aloud to the class. Then re-read it, this time asking students to listen for words, phrases, and illustrations that appeal to their sight, hearing, touch, taste, and smell.

Next, have students work in pairs using several picture books strong in setting. Give each pair one Senses Census template (Figure 2.1) to complete for each title. Students will report results to the class when they are finished.

Next, ask students to think about a place that appeals to their senses and have them write a description of it. When everyone is finished, students will exchange papers. Ask readers to evaluate for vivid overall descriptions, and have them circle the sense words and phrases. Then ask partners to discuss their work in light of their readers' opinions.

Site Analysis

NCTE 1, 2, 3, 4, 5, 6, 11, 12 Before builders can build, they must perform a site analysis to make sure the ground is stable, water will drain properly, and the environment will not be harmed. After students understand setting, have them perform a site analysis to see if the setting is a worthy one on which to build a story. Practice together as a class by reading a story with strong setting, such as *All the Way to Lhasa* by Barbara Helen Berger. Prepare a transparency of the Site Analysis template (Figure 2.2) and project it as you read. Read through the book page by page. Ask students for answers to the Site Analysis template, filling it in as you

FIGURE 2.1 **Senses Census**

Name(s) _____ Date _____

Book Title _____

In the appropriate box, copy words and phrases from the book that refer to the senses. You may have many for some senses and none for others.

Sight	Sound	Touch	Taste	Smell

read. An example is shown as Figure 2.3.

Next, students will work in pairs or small groups. Give each group a picture book with a strong sense of place. Have the groups analyze the setting by completing the Site Analysis template. When the groups have finished, they will report their findings orally to the class.

Variation

Instead of having groups report orally, ask them to prepare a written report summarizing their findings.

Extension

In looking at the art, students may notice that sometimes one picture covers two pages, and sometimes each page has a separate picture. Collaborate with the art teacher to help students learn how picture books are designed. Illustrator Web sites often provide such information, as well as illustrator contact information. See Barbara Helen Berger's Home Page (author and illustrator of *All the Way to Lhasa*) to learn more about her and her art <http://bhberger.com/>.

Placemat Places

| NCTE 1, 2, 3, 4, 5, 6, 11, 12 |

Collaborate with your art teacher for this activity. Have each student choose a picture book with a strong sense of place. Students will create placemats based on their books on 17 x 11 inch paper. Students should give an overall feeling of the book's setting and include pictures and words, either from the book or original descriptions. Laminate the placemats and have your class use them in the classroom or cafeteria after they have shown them to the rest of the class. When they are done using them as placemats at school, display them in the classroom or allow students to take them home.

The Setting-Plot Connection

| NCTE 1, 2, 3, 4, 5, 6, 11, 12 |

To help students see how setting influences plot (and vice versa), show students a wordless picture book, such as *Tuesday* by David Wiesner. Show each page long enough for students to take notes on setting. Then ask them to write descriptions of the settings as they appear in the book. Have them read their results in small groups, asking each other, "Does your description imply a plot?"

Extension

If the students answer "yes" to "Does your description imply a plot?", ask them to write their stories and share them with the class.

FIGURE 2.2 ## Site Analysis

Name(s) _____

Book Title _____

Complete the following template to do a page-by-page site analysis of the book.

PAGE	DESCRIBE PLACE	WHAT WORDS TELL	WHAT PICTURES TELL
1.			
2.			
3.			
4.			
5.			
6.			
7.			
8.			
9.			
10.			
11.			
12.			
13.			
14.			
15.			
16.			
17.			
18			
19.			
20.			
21.			
22.			
23.			
24.			
25.			
26.			
27.			
28.			
29.			
30			

FIGURE 2.3 Site Analysis Sample

Name(s) __Whole Class__ Date _____

Book Title __All the Way to Lhasa__

Complete the following template to do a page-by-page site analysis of the book.

PAGE	DESCRIBE PLACE	WHAT WORDS TELL	WHAT PICTURES TELL
1.	Tibet	name of place	mountainous, rural
2.	roadside	road to Lhasa	green grass
3.	same as above	same as above	dirty road
4.	same as above	same as above	same as above
5.	same as above	same as above	yak, native dress
6.	same as above	same as above	green grass, dusty road
7.	further up the road	same as above	higher elevations, steep trail
8.	same as above	windy, steep slope	elevation gain shown, flags fluttering in wind
9.	further along the road	torrents	higher elevation, mountain goats, raging river
10.	crossing a bridge	no text	raging river, crossing river on narrow bridge, flags fluttering
11.	yak carrying burdens through snow	no text	snow falling, clouds curling, yak plodding
12.	boy trudging through snow pulling yak	snow	snow, clouds, boy trudging, fox watching
13.	dark clouds	dark	monster face in darkclouds above yak's head
14.	further on the roads to Lhasa	road to Lhasa	snowy mountains with dark clouds moving in, boy with snow on hat

What's Happening?

NCTE 1, 2, 3, 4, 5, 6, 11, 12   Choose a picture book or books with a strong sense of place. Read one or more aloud to the class. Then ask the class to use their imaginations and write about what is happening at the story settings when the characters are not there. *Meanwhile Back at the Ranch* by Trinka Hakes Noble may be used as a model. Have students read their results aloud to the class or to small groups.

Wish You Were Here

NCTE 1, 2, 3, 4, 5, 6, 11, 12   Postcards often show interesting, beautiful places on one side and the line, "Wish you were here," written on the other. Collect and exhibit postcards for your class to see. Discuss what better lines you could write than "Wish you were here" that would make the place come alive for the reader. Read aloud *Stringbean's Trip to the Shining Sea* by Vera B. Williams and Jennifer Williams, and discuss the use and style of postcards. Then have students choose a picture book with a strong sense of place. Copy and distribute a Postcard template to each student (Figure 2.4). Use cardstock to simulate real postcards. Have students write a postcard to you making the place in their chosen book come alive. Have them draw a picture depicting the setting on the other side.

FIGURE 2.4   **Postcard**

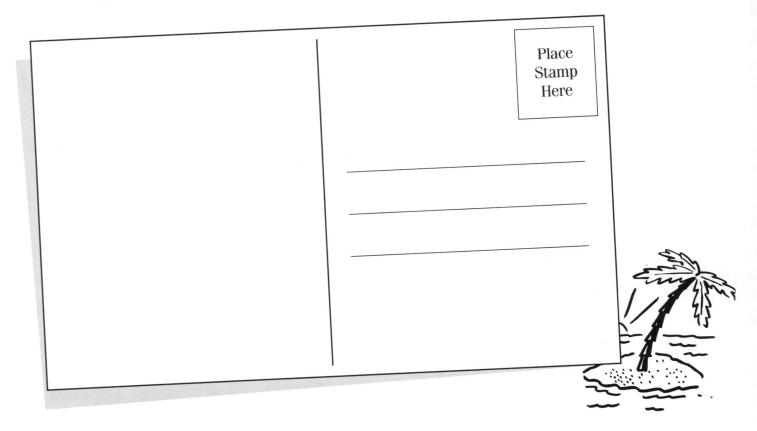

Picture Perfect

NCTE 1, 2, 3, 4, 11, 12 Choose a picture book with a strong sense of place, such as *Mountain Dance* by Thomas Locker, and read aloud to the class a descriptive passage. Do not show students the accompanying pictures. Ask students to draw the setting based on what you read. When students are finished, they will show their pictures either to the entire class or in small groups. Discuss differences and similarities. Then show the class the illustration that accompanied the passage you read. Ask, "Are any students' pictures similar? Did the writer give enough description to draw a picture?" You may point out that picture books may lack much physical description, allowing the artist to create it visually. Collaborate with the art teacher to help the class learn more about the art technique used in the book.

Time

The other main component of setting is when a story takes place. This includes historical period or year, season, month, day, and hour. To see the effect of time on how things look, do one or more of the following:

- Have students bring in baby pictures and recent pictures. Post them side-by-side to see the effects of time.
- Ask teachers to bring in baby pictures. Create a bulletin board in the library with the caption "Guess Who," and have a contest in which students guess the name of the teachers from the baby pictures.
- Choose an outdoor object you can see from the classroom. Have students record how the object looks in the morning, at midday, and late in the afternoon.
- On a sunny day, go outside and have students measure and record each other's shadows in the morning, at midday, and late in the afternoon.
- Plant a seed in a plastic cup. Observe it each day and record its growth.

These activities show how time changes things. Time in stories makes a difference, too. Read picture books set in different time periods and seasons. Discuss with the class the importance of that time period to that story.

Time Spin

NCTE 1, 2, 3, 4, 5, 6, 11, 12 Choose a picture book with a strong sense of time, such as *A Turkey for Thanksgiving* by Eve Bunting, or allow students to choose their own picture book from those you have selected. Then have them "spin" (write) the story into a different time period, season, or time of day. Ask them to read their results aloud to the class or in small groups. Discuss how much of the story changes.

Extension

Have students "spin" the same story one more time, setting it in yet another time.

Time Jump

NCTE 1, 2, 3, 4, 5, 6, 11, 12 Choose a picture book set in the past, such as *Pink and Say* by Patricia Polacco, and read it aloud to the class. Ask them how the story would be different if took place now. Then have them each write that story and share results aloud in small groups.

Time Traveler

NCTE 1, 2, 3, 4, 6, 11, 12 Develop students' awareness of inauthenticity of setting with this activity. Ask a student to look up "anachronism" in a dictionary. Brainstorm and record on the board examples of anachronisms, such as microwaves in pioneer days or cars in Shakespeare's time.

Read to the class a story set in the past, such as *My Great-Aunt Arizona* by Gloria Houston. Then have them work in groups to rewrite the story, inserting things from today into that world. Have groups read their finished stories aloud to the class.

Variations

- Rather than true anachronisms, have students insert inaccuracies by rewriting the story with things atypical to the story's season or time of day, such as snow in summer.
- Collaborate with the social studies teacher and the library media specialist to help students research the accuracy of an author's historical details.

Does Anybody Really Know What Time It Is?

NCTE 1, 2, 3, 4, 5, 6, 11, 12 This activity will show students how authors incorporate time into their stories and give them practice in doing the same. Have students work with a partner or in small groups. They will choose three books with a strong sense of time. Distribute three What Time Is It? templates (Figure 2.5) to each group. Have them share their findings with their classmates.

Extension

Have several pairs of dice available. Allow each student to shake a pair of dice twice, once for the hour and once for the month. Tell students to assume that the year is the present. Ask them to write a scene or short story set at that time. Have them share their results in small groups. Discuss any special challenges they had in writing about that time.

Split-Second Timing

NCTE 1, 2, 3, 4, 5, 6, 11, 12 Read a picture book aloud to the class, stopping after an important action has taken place. Ask the class, "What if this had happened one minute (or one day or one week) sooner or one minute later? How would the story be different?" Have students write the story with important events happening slightly ahead or behind what the author had in mind. Have students share results aloud in small groups.

FIGURE 2.5   **What Time Is It?**

Name(s) _____   Date _____

Book Title _____

Read the book and complete the chart below to find out what time it is.

	EVIDENCE	
	FROM WORDS	**FROM ILLUSTRATIONS**
Time Period, Historical Era, or Year		
Season or Month		
Time of Day		

So Tense!

NCTE 1, 2, 3, 4, 5, 6, 11, 12 Students should be able to properly understand and use the verb tenses past, present, and future. To introduce this activity, read aloud to the class several picture books with strong setting and ask them what verb tense is used. It will almost always be past tense. Ask students why they think this would be so. Then have each student choose a picture book with strong setting. Ask them to rewrite the book, changing the tense. If the tense is past, have them change it to present or future. Students will read their results aloud in small groups, with the audience listening for tense consistency and correcting errors. Discuss which tense is best for their particular stories and why.

Setting Shifts

NCTE 1, 2, 3, 4, 5, 6, 11, 12 Some picture books and most stories and books in general contain several scenes in several settings. To introduce this concept, choose a picture book with scene shifts in different settings, such as *Santa Calls* by Willam Joyce. Before you read it aloud to the class, ask students to watch and listen for shifts in time and place. Read the picture book, showing the pictures to the class as you read.

When you have finished, ask which setting shifts they noticed. Then students will work with partners or in small groups. They will choose a picture book with a strong setting. Copy and distribute Setting Shifts template (Figure 2.6) for groups to complete. Groups should report results to the class when the students are finished.

Extension

Have students insert a scene into the middle of the picture book they charted. The scene should be written in a different time and place than the previous and following scenes. Have students share their results aloud to the class or in small groups.

Transition Transport

NCTE 1, 2, 3, 4, 5, 6, 11, 12 Explain to students that transitions are words or phrases used to transport the reader smoothly from one scene to the next, just as a smooth flight easily takes a traveler from one city to another. A shift without transitions can be like a flight with air turbulence!

Use student results from Setting Shifts Discussion Question 2 (Figure 2.6) or read a picture book, such as *The Girl Who Loved Wild Horses* by Paul Goble, aloud to the class. Show the pictures as you read. Ask students to listen and watch for how the author and illustrator moved smoothly from one scene to the next. When you have completed the story, ask students for words, phrases, and pictures that helped them shift. Or have students write words and phrases down as you read. Talk about what the transitional words mean and how they work. Ask when you would use which words.

Next, prepare a text from a picture book, typing it without the transitional words and phrases, and leaving spaces between scenes. Copy and distribute this page to students and

FIGURE 2.6 # Setting Shifts

Name(s) _____   Date _____

Book Title _____

Complete the chart below by writing in order the changes in place and time in the story. Fill in only those rows that apply. (Your picture book may have fewer than five scenes). Add rows if your picture book has more than five scenes.

SCENE	PLACE	TIME
Scene 1		
Scene 2		
Scene 3		
Scene 4		
Scene 5		

Discuss these questions in your group:

1 What if the story had stayed in one place or one time?

2 How did the author and illustrator move smoothly from one setting to another?

have them write in the spaces the appropriate transitional words or phrases. Take care not to violate copyright. An alternate method is to cover the transitional text with opaque paper, read and show the book to students, asking them to state appropriate transitional words. Then read the actual text and have students compare their work with the original.

Picture Books with Strong Settings

Arnold, Katya. *Baba Yaga: A Russian Folktale*, New York: North South, 1993. A retelling of a traditional Baba Yaga tale, in which a little girl outsmarts the witch and escapes.

Bang, Molly. *Ten, Nine, Eight*, New York: Harper, Reissue ed., 1991. A little girl's room goes to bed to a lullaby containing numbers.

Barner, Bob. *Parade Day*, New York: Holiday House, 2003. A parade a month celebrates holidays throughout the year.

Baylor, Byrd. *If You Are a Hunter of Fossils*, Topeka, KS: Bt Bound, 1999. A fossil hunter describes what the west Texas mountain area might have been like eons ago.

_____. *I'm in Charge of Celebrations*, New York: Atheneum, 1986. Describes celebrating every day life in the desert.

_____. *The Way to Start A Day*, New York: Atheneum, 1978. Describes how people around the world greet the new day.

Beames, Margaret. *Night Cat*, New York: Orchard, 2003. Oliver, the cat, is excited with the opportunity to be outside at night until he gets scared and wants his indoor comforts.

Berger, Barbara Helen. *All the Way to Lhasa,* New York: Philomel, 2002. Retold Tibetan tale. A boy and his yak follow the advice of the old woman beside the road and reach Lhasa safely, even though others fail.

Bunting, Eve. *Smoky Night*, New York: Harcourt, 1994. The Los Angeles riots ripped neighborhoods apart, but this story tells about a boy and his family who learn how to come together with people who are different.

_____. *A Turkey for Thanksgiving*, New York: Clarion, 1991. Mr. and Mrs. Moose invite a turkey to their Thanksgiving feast. The turkey misunderstands, thinking he is the intended meal.

Burton, Virginia Lee. *The Little House*, Boston: Houghton, 1978. Shows changes in time, as a little house watches the city grow up around her.

Cannon, Janell. *Stellaluna*, New York: Harcourt, 1993. Stellaluna, a young bat, is separated from her mother and raised by birds. Stellaluna takes on birds' ways, even though she finds them odd. She is later reunited with her mother, who teaches her bat ways again. Stellaluna learns how to be friends with those who are different without sacrificing her own ways.

Daly, Niki. *Jamela's Dress,* New York: Farrar, 1999. Jamela takes her mother's expensive fabric through the streets of her South African town. Now what will her mother wear to the wedding she and Jamela are to attend?

Day, Alexander. *Carl Goes Shopping*, New York: Farrar, 1989. Carl, a big, black dog, is given instructions to take care of the baby while the baby's mother shops. Instead, Carl takes the baby on adventures in a department store, returning to mother just before she notices they were gone.

DeGroat, Diane. *Roses are Pink, Your Feet Really Stink,* Topeka, KS: Bt Bound, 1999. Gilbert forges names on mean Valentines and gets into trouble.

Feelings, Muriel. *Moja Means One,* Topeka, KS: Bt Bound, 1999. A Swahili counting book, the authors connect counting with things typical to East African life.

Felix, Monique. *The Wind*, New York: Stewart, 1991. A mouse learns about wind.

Fleischman, Paul. *Weslandia*, Cambridge, MA: Candlewick, 1999. Feeling that he does not fit in, Wesley creates his own land and becomes self-sufficient. His classmates are drawn to his new world.

Galdone, Paul. *The Three Bears*, New York: Clarion, 1979. Galdone's version of the traditional tale of a girl entering the bears' home and falling asleep in baby bear's bed.

Gerstein, Mordicai. *The Man Who Walked Between the Towers*, Brookfield, CT: Millbrook, 2003. In 1974, Philippe Petit walked on a high wire between the World Trade Center towers. This book commemorates the event, citing Petit's skill and courage, and paying tribute to the great towers.

_____. *Mountains of Tibet*, New York: Harper, 1987. A Tibetan woodcarver who can choose his reincarnation considers his many options and chooses a life very similar to the one he left.

Goble, Paul. *The Girl Who Loved Wild Horses,* Glenview, IL: Foresman, Reissue ed., 1993. A retold Native American tale. A girl loves her people, but loves the wild horses more. Her village releases her to them, and they run away together.

Hoban, Lillian. *Arthur's Great Big Valentine,* New York: HarperCollins, 1989. Arthur and his best friend are not getting along, but make up using special Valentines.

Hoestalándt, Jo. *Star of Fear, Star of Hope,* New York: Walker, 1995. In 1942 France, Helen's friend, Lydia, is forced to wear a Star of David. When Lydia leaves Helen's home before Helen's birthday party, Helen is so angry, she says that Lydia is no longer her friend. Helen narrates the story as an old woman full of regret for words spoken to a friend she never saw again.

Houston, Gloria. *My Great-Aunt Arizona*, New York: Harper, 1992. A true story, Arizona was born in the Blue Ridge Mountains in the 1800s. She longed to travel, but instead taught school in the school she had once attended, educating generations of Appalachian children about the wonderful places of the world.

Isadora, Rachel. *Ben's Trumpet*, New York: Greenwillow, 1979. A young boy growing up in the Jazz Age of the 1920s dreams of playing the trumpet. Professional jazzmen give him encouragement.

Johnston, Tony. *Alice Nizzy Nazzy: The Witch of Santa Fe*, New York: Putnam, 1995. A Southwest version of the traditional Russian Baba Yaga story, where a young girl outsmarts a witch, New Mexico style.

Joyce, William. *Santa Calls*, New York: HarperCollins, 1993. Art Aimesworth's sister gets the Christmas gift she requested from Santa, and Art, his sister, and their friend take an amazing trip to the North Pole.

Keats, Ezra Jack. *The Snowy Day*, New York: Viking, 1962. A little boy experiences a snowy day in the city.

Kimmel, Eric. *Hershel and the Hanukkah Goblins*, New York: Holiday House, 1989. A retold Jewish tale in which Hershel outsmarts the goblins that haunt the synagogue and prevent the people from celebrating Hanukkah.

Lester, Julius. *Black Cowboy, Wild Horses*, New York: Dial 1988. A true story of a black cowboy who relates to horses so that they do what he wants.

Lewin, Betsy. *What's the Matter, Habibi?,* Boston: Houghton, 1997. Habibi, the camel, gives rides to children for his master, Ahmed, until Habibi becomes discontented. Ahmed tries to find out what is wrong, and learns that it is nothing that a trip to the bazaar cannot fix.

Lobato, Arcadio. *The Secret of the North Pole*, New York: McGraw, 2003. Peter, a little polar bear, finds a red hat in the snow and returns it to the North Pole, where he learns the secret of how Santa can deliver toys around the world in one night.

Locker, Thomas. *Mountain Dance*, San Diego: Harcourt, 2001. Tells poetically how different kinds of mountains are formed.

_____. *Walking with Henry*, Golden, CO: Fulcrum, 2002. An imaginary trip into the wilderness introduces readers to Henry David Thoreau and his writings.

_____. *Where the River Begins*, Topeka, KS: Bt Bound, 1993. Two boys and their grandfather camp out and try to find the source of a river.

London, Jonathan. *Froggy Gets Dressed*, Topeka, KS: Bt Bound, 1999. Froggy is so eager to play in the snow that he forgets to get fully dressed. His mother calls him back to put on what he forgot.

Martin, Jacqueline Briggs. *Snowflake Bentley,* Boston: Houghton, 1998. A biography of W.A. Bentley, a scientist who photographed snowflakes to study their formations.

Mayer, Mercer. *Frog Goes to Dinner,* Topeka, KS: Bt Bound, 1999. Frog jumps from the pocket in which he hid and disrupts dinner in a fancy restaurant.

_____. *Frog, Where Are You?,* Topeka, KS: Bt Bound, 1999. Frog escapes. He is tracked by a boy and his dog.

_____. *Liza Lou and the Yeller Belly Swamp*, Topeka, KS: Bt Bound, 1999. Liza Lou outsmarts all the monsters of the Yeller Belly Swamp.

McCloskey, Robert. *Make Way for Ducklings*, New York: Viking, 1941. Mr. and Mrs. Mallard bring their duck family to the Boston Public Garden.

McLerran, Alice. *Roxaboxen,* New York: Harper, 1991. Children make up magical play and places by using a box and rocks on a hillside.

McPhail, David, *Farm Morning*, Topeka, KS: Bt Bound, 1999. Father and daughter feed all the farm animals in the early morning.

Moss, Marissa. *True Heart*, New York: Silver Whistle, 1999. A young woman gets her heart's desire by engineering a train after the real engineer is injured. Set in the late 1800s-early 1900s.

Noble, Trinka Hakes. *The Day Jimmy's Boa Ate the Wash,* New York: Penguin, 1980. Jimmy's class takes a field trip to a farm—with Jimmy's boa. The boa causes all kinds of chaos.

_____. *Meanwhile Back at the Ranch*, Topeka, KS: Bt Bound, 1999. A bored rancher goes to town in search of excitement, never imagining the excitement that is happening back home in his absence.

Nye, Naomi Shihab. *Sitti's Secrets*, Topeka, KS: Bt Bound, 1999. Mona visits her Palestinian grandmother on the West Bank.

Polacco, Patricia. *Pink and Say*, New York: Philomel, 1994. Based on a true story, black Union soldier, Pink, finds injured white soldier, Say, takes him home, and, with the help of his mother, nurses Say back to health. They develop a strong friendship. Both are taken to Andersonville where Pink is hanged.

Priceman, Marjorie. *How to Make an Apple Pie and See the World*, New York: Random, 1994. A girl who wants to make an apple pie is undeterred by a closed market. She travels the world, going to the place of origin for essential ingredients to bake her pie.

Rylant, Cynthia. *When I Was Young in the Mountains*, New York: Dutton, 1982. An autobiographical story about the pleasures of growing up in the mountains.

Say, Allen. *Grandfather's Journey*, Boston, MA: Houghton, 1993. Grandfather's journey begins in Japan and ends in the U.S. Grandfather loves both countries and instills that love in his children and grandchildren, so that they make the journey between countries, too.

Seuling, Barbara. *Winter Lullaby,* New York: Browndeer, 1998. Shows how a variety of creatures spend the winter.

Sharmat, Marjorie Wienman. *Gila Monsters Meet You at the Airport*, Glenview, IL: Foresman, 1980. A boy moves from New York City to Arizona, where everything is strange and new.

Shulevitz, Uri. *Snow*, New York: Farrar, 1998. A boy and his dog believe the city's snowfall will be big.

Sis, Peter. *Madlenka*, New York: Francis Foster, 2000. Madlenka lives in New York City. She shows her friend that people from around the world live on her block.

Soto, Gary. *Too Many Tamales*, New York: Putnam, 1993. Mother and daughters gather to make tamales for the Christmas Eve feast. Maria puts on her mother's wedding ring and loses it. She thinks it is in the tamale dough. Her cousins help look for the ring by eating tamales, only to find the truth.

Stanley, Diane. *Saving Sweetness*, New York: Putnam, 1996. The sheriff, who is telling the story, tells readers how he saved the little orphan, Sweetness. The pictures show the truth.

Tamar, Erika. *The Garden of Happiness*, New York: Harcourt, 1996. Marisol and her neighbors transform a New York City vacant lot into a lush garden.

Ward, Lynd. *The Biggest Bear*, Boston: Houghton, 1952. Johnny is determined to find and kill the biggest bear so that its skin can hang on the wall. Instead, he finds a bear that he wants to keep as a pet. It causes too much trouble and must be put away—fortunately in the zoo.

Van Allsburg, Chris. *The Polar Express*, Boston: Houghton, 1985. Christmas Eve, a magical train ride to the North Pole, and a special gift from Santa—what more could anyone want?

Weitzman, Jacqueline Preiss and Robin Preiss Glasser. *You Can't Take a Balloon into the Metropolitan Museum,* New York: Dial, 1998. A girl and her grandmother visit the Metropolitan Museum. The girl must leave her balloon at the entrance. It escapes and has adventures while the girl and her grandmother view the art.

Wellington, Monica. *Night City*, New York: Dutton, 1998. What happens in the city after the sun goes down? Who works while most of the city sleeps?

Wiesner, David. *Sector 7*, New York: Clarion, 1999. A boy on a visit to the Empire State Building is taken by a cloud and shown the cloud dispersion system.

_____. *Tuesday*, New York: Clarion, 1991. A few introductory words lead to the wordless story of frogs flying on lily pads and zooming through neighborhoods while people sleep.

Williams, Vera B. and Jennifer Williams. *Stringbean's Trip to the Shining Sea,* NY: Morrow, 1988. Written in the form of postcards, a boy and his big brother take a road trip to the Pacific Ocean.

Wood, Audrey. *King Bidgood's in the Bathtub,* New York: Harcourt, 1985. The King is in the bathtub. The members of his court plead, but he succeeds in getting them into the tub, too. The King will not come out until a young page pulls the drain plug.

_____. *The Napping House,* New York: Harcourt, 1984. Everyone in the house piles onto the bed and naps until a wakeful flea upsets the peace.

Wright, Betty Ren. *The Blizzard,* New York: Holiday, 2003. Billy is disappointed that a blizzard prevents his cousins from coming to his birthday party, but he has a party anyway, when his family takes in Billy's classmates and teacher.

Yolen, Jane, *Owl Moon,* New York: Philomel, 1987. A poetically told story about a father and daughter hiking into the woods at night and calling a great horned owl.

CHAPTER

Plot 3

Defining plot is simple. Plot is the action of the story. Plot is what happens. Learning and applying effective plotting techniques to engage readers is much more difficult than the definition would indicate. This chapter will give young writers practice in studying and creating strong plots.

In Good Order

NCTE 1, 2, 3, 4, 5, 6, 11, 12 The action of the story must occur in proper order for it to make sense and have its fullest impact. Writers must think, "What does the reader need to know now?" Have students practice their sequencing skills with this small group activity, taking care to comply with federal copyright law.

Type the text of a picture book, an original story, or traditional folktale with strong plot. Cut the text apart by page. Put strips in a manila envelope labeled with the book's title. Make as many envelopes as you have groups, either using the same story or different stories for each. Distribute the envelopes to the groups and have them put the strips in the correct plot order. Then have them read the corresponding picture book to check their work. If you have made envelopes containing different stories, rotate them through the groups.

Variation

Prepare as above. Distribute the envelopes to the groups, with each student drawing a strip until all strips are taken. Working within the group, students determine sequence. When all groups are ready, each group will stand in order and read its sentences, thus reading the story.

Extension

After students have assembled the story correctly, have them write a silly out-of-order version and share aloud with their small group.

And Then What?

NCTE 1, 2, 3, 4, 5, 6, 11, 12   Surprise is one aspect of plotting that pleases readers. Readers may think they have correctly predicted a plot outcome, but are delighted when the writer inserts a believable twist. When creating plots, the writer must be aware of a logical flow of events, or sequencing, but must also work to provide surprise. At every point in the plot, the writer must consider not only the obvious possibilities, but also the less obvious. The writer must constantly ask, "And then what?" This activity will give students practice in providing surprise.

Choose a picture book with a strong plot, such as *Jimmy's Boa and the Bungee Jump Slam Dunk* by Trinka Hakes Noble. Decide in advance where crucial action takes place, and stop reading on the page before that action (or stop after every two pages). Then ask the class, "And then what happens?" Write (or have a student write) their responses on the board. Continue reading and comparing the author's plot to the students' suggestions. Read again until just before the next crucial action and repeat asking, recording, reading, and comparing. Leave all recordings on the board, to be used later. Continue until the book is finished. Discuss whether the story contained any surprises, whether it is believable and whether the outcome was satisfying. Even fantasy must be constructed in a believable world.

Next ask students to rewrite the story, beginning with the story's beginning, but changing the story by using one or more of the ideas on the board from their predictions. When everyone is finished, students will share aloud in small groups. Have them complete the And Then What? template (Figure 3.1) to evaluate each other's stories. Conclude by conducting a general class discussion about what the students learned.

Ready, Set, Go

NCTE 1, 2, 3, 4, 5, 6, 11, 12   This activity helps students focus on a story's action. Have students work with a partner or in small groups. Each group will choose a picture book with a strong plot. Copy and distribute a Ready, Set, Go template (Figure 3.2) to each group. Students will create a board game based on the plot of their book. Provide general art supplies for them to decorate their boards. (If students are unfamiliar with board games, show them a common one, such as Chutes and Ladders, Candy Land, Sorry, or Monopoly. Demonstrate how the game is played, so they have an understanding of the rules and components.)

Help students make spinners or provide dice for moving spaces. Use beans or paper clips as game markers. When groups have perfected their games, they will glue the templates onto cardboard or card stock. Then have them write the rules for their game.

When the groups are ready, they will present their games to the class. Allow time for students to rotate through the games. Keep them for classroom use or give them to a primary grade classroom to accompany the books on which they are based.

Extension

For a more sophisticated game, have groups apply And Then What? to their chosen picture books. Ask groups to make their board game show choices based on those responses, so the game could have a different ending each time.

FIGURE 3.1

And Then What?

Name(s) _____

Evaluate your groups' stories by completing the chart below.

Story Writer's Name	Was there surprise? If so, WHAT?	Is story believable? WHY?	Is the outcome satisfying? WHY?

FIGURE 3.2 **Ready, Set, Go**

In each space write something that happened in the story. Then create a game for two or more players.

THE

_____
(Name of Book)

GAME

Let It Flow

NCTE 1, 2, 3, 4, 7, 11, 12 This activity promotes logical thinking by showing students how to apply cause and effect logic to their stories. Begin by explaining cause and effect. When one event happens, it causes another event to happen or sets another series of events in motion. This can sometimes be expressed with "If...then" statements. Practice a few with your class, such as, "If plants receive the right amount of sun and water, then....," "If drinking water is contaminated, then...." Allow students to make their own "If...then" statements, with the class considering whether the cause and effect elements are actually related. ("If Sally wears a sweater, then it will rain" is illogical.)

Flow charts are used to show processes and their connections. In this activity, a flow chart will show story events and their connections. Students may be unfamiliar with flow charts. Make a transparency of the Let It Flow template (Figure 3.3), project it on an overhead projector, and complete it as a class. *If You Take a Mouse to School* by Laura Numeroff or other books in her series work well for this.

Have students work with a partner or in small groups. Each group will choose a picture book with a strong plot. Copy and distribute the Let It Flow template (Figure 3.3), and have students make a flow chart of the story's main events. Groups will share their results upon completion.

Extension

Have students use the flow chart or a flow chart variation to create a story in which readers choose the story's outcome. (See sample on page 56, Figure 3.4.) Large rolls of butcher paper work well for this. Students will need to consider several plotting options, as they did in the And Then What? exercise. Have them choose the three strongest options and insert them as choices. Have them continue the plot from each choice, inserting as many choices along the way as they like. The finished product should contain at least three different stories, if readers follow each plot all the way through.

Beginnings

Ask students if they have ever put a book or story down after reading only the first paragraph. Then ask why. A good story beginning usually introduces characters, setting, and plot in such an interesting way that readers want to continue. The first sentence may or may not contain the problem, but the problem is introduced in the first few paragraphs.

In the Beginning

NCTE 1, 2, 3, 4, 5, 6, 11, 12 To help students understand good beginnings, have them study some appropriate picture books, choosing from the list of Picture Books with Strong Plots or from favorites. They will read only the first sentence of several picture books with strong plots. As they read, they will copy the sentences or first paragraphs onto the In the Beginning template (Figure 3.5).

FIGURE 3.3 # Let It Flow

Name(s) _____ Date _____

Write main events in order in the boxes below. Draw arrows connecting the boxes to show the flow of events. Draw dotted arrow lines to show what event caused another event.

Book Title _____

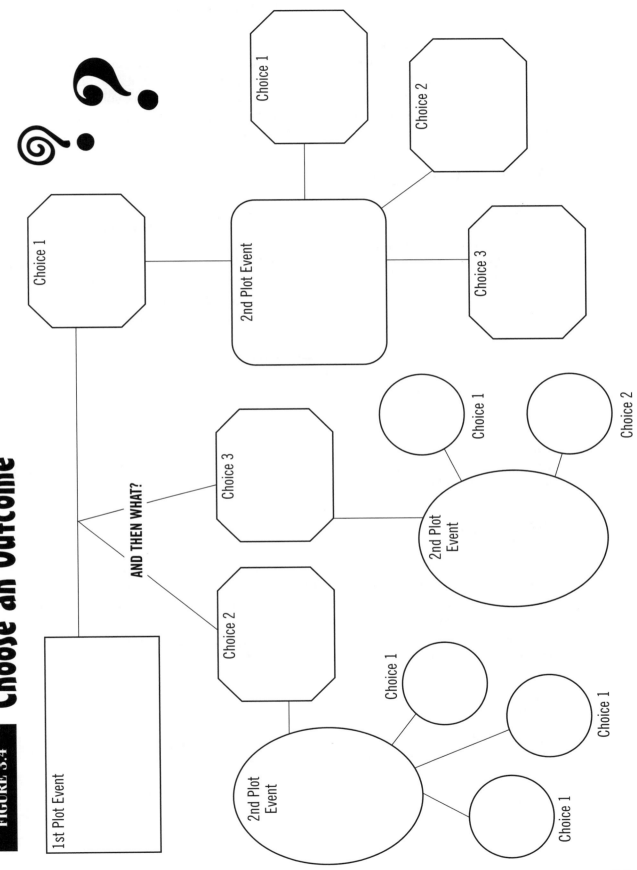

FIGURE 3.4 Choose an Outcome

1st Plot Event

AND THEN WHAT?

Choice 1

Choice 2

Choice 3

2nd Plot Event

Choice 1

Choice 2

Choice 3

2nd Plot Event

Choice 1

Choice 2

2nd Plot Event

Choice 1

Choice 1

Choice 1

When students have completed the template, have them write a numeral 1 beside the beginning they liked best, 2 beside the one they liked next best, and so on. Then they will discuss in small groups why they liked which beginnings. Next, they will try to improve the beginnings they liked least, writing those on the back of their templates. Working individually, they will write stories based on one of the beginnings they copied. Students will share their stories aloud in small groups, with some volunteers reading to the entire class. Encourage students to read the entire picture book of the beginning they chose to see if their stories are similar to the authors' books.

A Good Beginning

| NCTE 1, 2, 3, 4, 5, 6, 11, 12 |

A good beginning (first sentence or first paragraph) should introduce characters, setting, and problem. Common methods for beginnings include narrative description of setting (*Borreguita and the Coyote* by Verna Aardema), narrative description of character (*Lilly's Purple Plastic Purse* by Kevin Henkes), dialogue (*Dr. De Soto* by William Steig), and first person character introduction (*A Chair for My Mother* by Vera B. Williams). Some begin immediately with the problem (*Click, Clack, Moo: Cows that Type* by Doreen Cronin). Have students evaluate picture book beginnings by working with partners to complete the A Good Beginning template (Figure 3.6).

Have students share their findings in small groups. Then write their own stories using one of these techniques.

Extension

For more work on beginnings, have students rewrite the story beginning they wrote in the previous exercise using a different technique. Discuss with them how it changed the story, and which beginning is stronger.

Middles

The largest part of the picture book or story is the middle. The middle develops the characters and the problem and explores possible solutions. This is also the hardest part to write. Many writers know how their story should begin and end, but the middle may require a lot of work to get the conflict, pacing, and obstacles right.

The library media specialist can help students find author interviews and articles that tell about their problems with writing middles.

Conflict

Every story has at least one conflict or problem. Otherwise, there would not be a story. The main types of conflict will be explored in the following sections.

FIGURE 3.5 # In the Beginning

Name(s) _____ Date _____

Book Title _____

First Sentence or Paragraph: _____

_____

_____

Book Title _____

First Sentence or Paragraph: _____

_____

_____

Book Title _____

First Sentence or Paragraph: _____

_____

_____

Book Title _____

First Sentence or Paragraph: _____

_____

_____

Book Title _____

First Sentence or Paragraph: _____

_____

_____

FIGURE 3.6

A Good Beginning

Name(s) _____ Date _____

Learn how picture book authors write story beginnings. Write the book title. In the other columns, write the page number on which this element is introduced.

BOOK TITLE	INTRODUCE CHARACTER	INTRODUCE SETTING	INTRODUCE PROBLEM	DESCRIPTION	DIALOGUE	FIRST PERSON CHARACTER	OTHER (WRITE WHAT)

Action-Reaction

One of the laws of physics states that for every action, there is an equal and opposite reaction. Character vs. character conflict is an example of that law, since what one character does ensures a reaction by the other character. Choose a picture book with character vs. character conflict and read it aloud to the class, showing the pictures as you read. Then identify the conflict step by step. Help students recognize cause and effect in the conflict. Then discuss how the conflict was resolved.

Next, students will work with partners, choosing a picture book with character vs. character conflict. Distribute the Action-Reaction template (Figure 3.7) for partners to complete. They will share their results in small groups when everyone is finished.

Character vs. Character

Two characters have a problem with each other in character vs. character conflict. A few books with character vs. character conflict are:

Alice Nizzy Nazzy: The Witch of Santa Fe by Tony Johnston

Borreguita and the Coyote by Verna Aardema

Click, Clack, Moo: Cows that Type Doreen Cronin

The Three Little Wolves and the Big Bad Pig by Eugene Trivizas

Extension

Have students write a scene (or two or three) of character vs. character conflict. Cause and effect relationships should be clear and believable. Have students share their work aloud in small groups, with volunteers reading to the entire class.

And the Winner Is

The main character has a problem that needs to be solved or a goal that needs to be reached. At the end of the book, the main character is usually successful. Choose a picture book with character vs. character conflict and read it aloud to the class. Discuss what the main character has solved or gained at the end of the story. Did the character in conflict with the main character lose anything so that the main character could win? (Some stories have resolutions where everyone wins.)

Next, have students rewrite the story so that the character in conflict with the main character wins. In other words, that character reaches the goal, not the main character. Have students share their work aloud in small groups or read aloud to the entire class.

It's All in the Motivation

Explain to students that people are motivated by different things. Ask students what motivates them. What makes them do the things they do? Ask by show of hands how many would prefer as a reward 1) going to a movie, 2) eating a pizza, 3) a day without homework. Then ask by show of hands, how many would consider the same things punishment. (If no one considers your choices punishment, ask if students know people who do not like going to movies or eating pizza and who do like homework.) Point out that because people have different likes and dislikes, they are motivated by different things.

FIGURE 3.7 # Action-Reaction

Name(s) _____ Date _____

Book Title _____

Names of Characters in Conflict: _____

Why don't these characters get along? In the chart below, write what each character does to the other to create and continue the conflict. In the bottom box, write the resolution to the conflict.

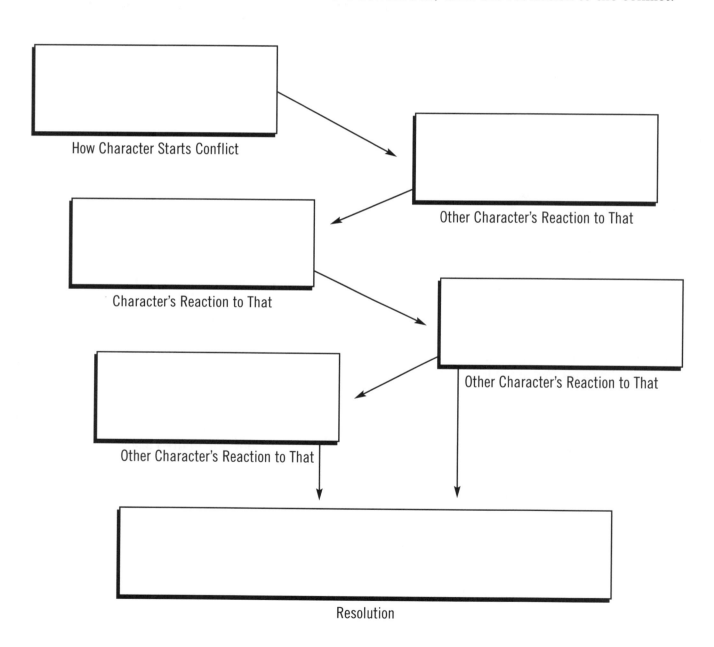

How Character Starts Conflict

Other Character's Reaction to That

Character's Reaction to That

Other Character's Reaction to That

Other Character's Reaction to That

Resolution

To make character conflict believable, a writer must understand the characters well enough to know why they do what they do. (See Chapter One: Character.) This activity will help students consider characters' motivations. Copy and distribute the It's All in the Motivation template (Figure 3.8). Have students work with partners or in small groups, choosing a picture book with character vs. character conflict. They will complete the template and report results to the class.

How Forceful

NCTE 1, 2, 3, 4, 5, 6, 11, 12

Students are probably familiar with Gary Paulsen's books or TV shows or movies that contain this type of conflict. Discuss what students know about character vs. nature conflict. Read aloud a picture book with character vs. nature conflict and discuss how the character overcame nature's force.

Have students work with partners or in small groups to examine several picture books containing character vs. nature conflict. Copy and distribute the How Forceful template (Figure 3.9) and have students complete. Have them join with another group and share their results. After this activity, ask the class what common traits they notice in character vs. nature stories.

Extension

Have students write a scene or story containing character vs. nature conflict and share aloud in small groups.

Natural Disaster Prevention

NCTE 1, 2, 3, 4, 5, 6, 7, 8, 11, 12

Students will choose one of the books they examined in How Forceful or another picture book containing character vs. nature conflict. Collaborate with the science teacher and library media specialist to help students find resources about the natural force that is part of the book's conflict. Then students will write letters to the main character telling the character what to do in this kind of situation or how to avoid this kind of situation.

Variation

Have students write letters to the editor of the school or local newspaper explaining the natural force that is part of the book's conflict. Students will tell what to do when such a situation occurs or how to avoid this kind of situation.

FIGURE 3.8 It's All in the Motivation

Name(s) _____   Date _____

Book Title _____

Read the book and complete the chart below to find out what the character's motivation.

NAME OF CHARACTER:	NAME OF CHARACTER:
Started conflict by doing because	Reacted to action by doing because
Reacted to other character by because	Reacted to other character by because
Contributed to resolution by because	Contributed to resolution by because

FIGURE 3.9 **How Forceful**

Name(s) _____ Date _____

Choose three picture books containing character vs. nature conflict. Complete the chart below to show traits of that type of conflict.

BOOK TITLE	NATURAL FORCE	HOW CHARACTER OVERCAME

Character vs. Society

Character vs. society conflict occurs when the character has problems with institutions or societal laws and mores. Some examples of picture books with character vs. society conflict are:

David Goes to School by David Shannon

Fly Away Home by Eve Bunting

Weslandia by Paul Fleischman

You Can Fight City Hall

| NCTE 1, 2, 3, 4, 5, 6, 7, 11, 12 |

Introduce character vs. society conflict by defining it and asking, "Which is more likely to change, the character or society?" Then read aloud a picture book containing character vs. society conflict. Ask students how the question was answered in this book.

Working with partners or in small groups, students will choose a picture book containing character vs. society conflict. Have students identify the conflict and discuss whether the societal element should be changed, and if so, how. Collaborate with your social studies teacher to help students learn how to make changes within institutions. If students decide that the societal element should change, have them write a letter to the appropriate person (principal, government official, company president) explaining the problem, the need for change, and how to make the change. If students decide the character should change, have them write the character a letter explaining the benefits of adapting to society and how to do so. Have students share their completed letters with other groups.

A New World Coming

| NCTE 1, 2, 3, 4, 5, 6, 11, 12 |

Working with partners or in small groups, students will choose a picture book containing character vs. society conflict. Students will identify the conflict and work together to rewrite the story. In this story, students should create a society in which the character's problem would not exist. Have them consider the effects on the larger story world, as well as creating a different conflict. Have them share their stories with the class.

Character vs. Self

Character vs. self conflict occurs in stories in which the character is his or her own enemy. A few books with character vs. character conflict are:

Lilly's Purple Plastic Purse by Kevin Henkes

The Great Gracie Chase by Cynthia Rylant

Owen by Kevin Henkes

Me vs. Me

| NCTE 1, 2, 3, 5, 6, 11, 12 |

Read to the class a picture book with character vs. self conflict. Discuss how the character was his or her own enemy. Did the resolution to the conflict show character growth? Ask students to think of a time when they fought against themselves and have them write a journal entry about it. Have them include what they learned and how they overcame the problem. Volunteers may share their entries.

Mirror, Mirror

NCTE 1, 2, 3, 4, 5, 6, 11, 12 | Character vs. self conflict is often expressed through a character's inner thoughts. Students will choose a picture book containing character vs. self conflict. Ask them to read the book, focusing on the conflict. Copy and distribute the Mirror, Mirror template (Figure 3.10). Have students imagine and write what the character would say if the character were speaking to his or her image in the mirror. Students will share results in small groups.

Pros and Cons

NCTE 1, 2, 3, 4, 5, 6, 12 | Working with partners, students will choose a picture book with character vs. self conflict. Copy and distribute the Pros and Cons template (Figure 3.11) to partners. Have students read the book and identify the conflict by completing the Pros and Cons template.

Then ask each student to write a friendly letter to the main character, recommending a course of action with reasons why. The outcome can be the same or different from the one in the picture book.

My Own Worst Enemy

NCTE 1, 2, 3, 4, 5, 6, 11, 12 | This activity promotes problem solving and critical thinking. Ask students if they have ever felt like their own worst enemies, as if everything they did was wrong. Characters in stories with character vs. self conflict may feel the same way.

Choose a book with character vs. self conflict and read it to the class, asking them to focus on the conflict. When you are finished reading, discuss the ways in which the character created or compounded his or her problems.

Then go through the book again, page by page. Ask students to identify the first indication of conflict. Write it (or have a student write it) on the board. Have students brainstorm what the character should do next and record their responses. Go through this list one item at a time and ask, "If the character does this, what will happen next?" Continue with the next indication of conflict and so on until you have finished the book. Leave the class's responses on the board.

Discuss how many different stories could have been written, but that the author chose to write it this way. Ask the class to consider why. Then have students write their own story based on their brainstorming and problem solving. They will share their stories aloud with the class and compare them with the original picture book. This activity is also effective with small groups.

FIGURE 3.10 # Mirror, Mirror

Name(s) _____ Date _____

Book Title _____

Imagine that the main character is talking to himself or herself while looking in the mirror. What would the character say about his or her conflict? Write your answer in the mirror below.

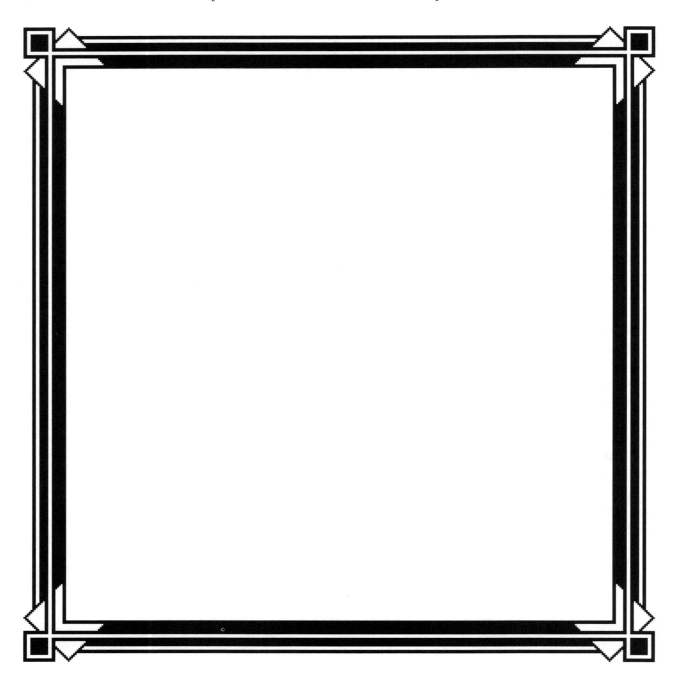

FIGURE 3.11   Pros and Cons

Name(s) _____   Date _____

Book Title _____

Character's Problem: _____

What does the character choose to do?_____

_____

List below the pros (good points) and cons (bad points) about the character's decision.

PROS	CONS

Problem + Solution = Plot

Conflict Comet

NCTE 1, 2, 3, 4, 5, 6, 8, 11, 12   Bring in several newspapers and have students count the number of stories containing conflict. Conflict makes news! Your class can create the *Conflict Comet* newspaper. Collaborate with the technology teacher or library media specialist to create a newspaper template using computer word processing or desktop publishing software.

Working with partners, students should choose a picture book with a strong plot and rewrite the story like a news story. They can use real newspapers as samples. Check their finished stories for errors, allow them to revise as needed, and key the story into the template.

When all groups have finished, print copies of the *Conflict Comet* for the class. You could also post the newspaper to your school Web site.

Writing How-To articles

NCTE 1, 2, 3, 4, 5, 6, 11, 12   Writing how-to articles helps students think and write logically and reinforces problem-solving skills. Show students samples of how-to articles (especially popular in craft and home oriented magazines). Discuss the information included and the format. How-to articles are often written in lists or steps.

Students will choose a picture book with strong plot. They will identify the conflict and think about how they would solve it. Then ask them to write a how-to article on solving the conflict. Have them share results aloud in small groups. Listeners should evaluate each article based on clarity, thoroughness, and practicality.

Extension

With revision, the best articles could be submitted for publication. The library media specialist can find journals that publish student submissions. Many magazines for young people call for student material. Other magazines accepting student work are listed in the "Young Writer's & Illustrator's Markets" chapter of *Children's Writer's & Illustrator's Market*, an annual publication.

Cooking Up Plots

NCTE 1, 2, 3, 4, 5, 6, 7, 11, 12   Show students sample recipes, emphasizing their unique format. Make a transparency of the Cooking Up Plots template (Figure 3.12) and project it on an overhead projector. Work together to write a recipe on the board, white board, or overhead transparency. See page 71 for an example.

Students will choose a picture book with strong plot. Copy and distribute Cooking Up Plots templates (Figure 3.12). Then have students write a recipe based on the plot. Suggestions are "A Recipe for Trouble," "A Recipe for Fun," "A Recipe for Confusion," and so on.

Students will write their final version on index cards and put them in a file box alphabetically by book title or author. Keep the box of cards in the classroom or library for students to read.

Book Title   The Three Little Wolves and the Big Bad Pig

Book Author   Eugene Triviza

A Recipe for Home Construction

Ingredients:
1 wheelbarrow
21 sticks, 5 ft. tall
Rope

Enough of each of the following to cover a wall:

Marigolds
Daffodils
Pink roses

Cherry blossoms
Enough Sunflowers to cover the ceiling
Enough Daisies to cover the floor

Preparation:
Put 4 sticks in ground, creating 5 ft. square. Use rope to tie sticks lengthwise across the tops of the first 4 sticks. Make "A" shape with 2 sticks and tie to top of front cross-bar for roof. Make "A" shape with 2 more sticks and tie to top of back cross-bar for roof. Make "A" shape with 2 sticks and tie to middle cross-bar for roof. Use wheel-barrow to haul loads of flowers, as indicated above. Attach to house by twisting stems together. Move in.

Variations

- Rather than writing index cards, students may use a word processing computer program to enter them into a template in the computer.

- Publish a class Picture Book Recipes book by using a word processing computer program to enter the recipes, printing and binding the finished work, and shelving in the classroom or library.

Obstacle Course

NCTE 1, 2, 3, 4, 5, 6, 11, 12 In the middle of a story, the character meets obstacle after obstacle on the way to solving the problem or reaching the goal. A reader should think, "It can't get any worse," and then it does. The author must be careful to put characters into situations that they can get out of.

Give students practice at throwing obstacles at characters with this activity. Choose a picture book with strong plot and read it aloud to the class. *It Could Always Be Worse: A Yiddish Tale* by Margot Zemach is one example. Ask students to identify the obstacles the character faces. Next, students will work with partners or in small groups. Copy and distribute the Obstacle Course template (Figure 3.13) to each group. They will choose several picture books with strong plots and complete the Obstacle Course template. Groups will report results to the class.

FIGURE 3.12 # Cooking Up Plots

Name(s) _____   Date _____

Book Title _____

Complete the form below to help you write a recipe based on the plot of the picture book you have chosen.

Recipe

Book Title _____

Book Author _____

A Recipe for _____

Ingredients:

Preparation:

Have students use scissors to cut apart the obstacle segments from their templates. Put them in a container. Students will each select three and write a story using the obstacles they have selected. Ask them to share their stories aloud in small groups or with the entire class.

Pacing

Pacing is important in plotting because it keeps things moving at a proper speed. Action scenes usually read faster than emotional scenes. Scenes with character introspection are usually slower than scenes with dialogue. Help students discover how to recognize and accomplish proper pacing with the activities that follow.

Mark the Speed Limit

| NCTE 1, 2, 3, 4, 5, 6, 11, 12 |

Copy the Speed Limit template (Figure 3.14), making at least four for every two students. Working with partners, students will choose a picture book with a strong plot. Students will cut apart speed limit bookmarks. Ask students to decide what the speed limit of each scene is and write the number on the templates, inserting them into the book like bookmarks. Make a chart on the board or large writing pad with three columns: Slow, Medium, Fast.

When everyone is finished, ask students to read examples of 70 mile per hour scenes (or other fast scenes). Ask what students notice about them. How are they alike? Write responses on the board in the Fast column. Continue through Medium and Slow speed limits, recording responses. Compare and contrast each type of scene: fast, medium, and slow. List differences and similarities.

Next, working with partners, students will rewrite a slow scene making it fast or a fast scene making it slow. Have two sets of partners read their results aloud to each other.

Endings

A book or story's ending is critical, as it is the last word a writer has with a reader. At the end of a book or story, the problem is usually resolved or there is a hint of resolution, and the main character has changed, grown, and developed. A good ending leaves the reader feeling satisfied. It may not be "happily ever after," but it should give the sense that this ought to be the way things end.

In the End

| NCTE 1, 2, 3, 4, 5, 6, 11, 12 |

This activity is similar to In the Beginning. To help students understand good endings, they should study some, choosing from the list of Picture Books with Strong Plots or from favorites. Ask them to read only the last sentence of several picture books with strong plots. As they read, have them copy the sentences or last paragraphs onto the In the End template (Figure 3.15).

FIGURE 3.13 **Obstacle Course**

Name(s) _____

Identify the obstacles the character must face and complete the chart below.

Book Title	Obstacle 1	Obstacle 2	Obstacle 3	Obstacles you can think of that the author did not include

FIGURE 3.14 # Speed Limit Template

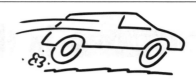

SPEED LIMIT	SPEED LIMIT	SPEED LIMIT	SPEED LIMIT	SPEED LIMIT
SPEED LIMIT	SPEED LIMIT	SPEED LIMIT	SPEED LIMIT	SPEED LIMIT

FIGURE 3.15 **In the End**

Name(s) _____ Date _____

Book Title _____

Last Sentence or Paragraph: _____

_____

_____

Book Title _____

Last Sentence or Paragraph: _____

_____

_____

Book Title _____

Last Sentence or Paragraph: _____

_____

_____

Book Title _____

Last Sentence or Paragraph: _____

_____

_____

Book Title _____

Last Sentence or Paragraph: _____

_____

The End!

_____

When students have completed the template, ask them to write a numeral 1 beside the ending they liked best, 2 beside the one they liked next best, and so on. Ask them to try to improve the endings they liked least, writing those on the back of their templates.

Working individually, students will write stories based on one of the endings they copied. They will share their stories aloud in small groups, with some volunteers reading to the entire class. Encourage students to read the entire picture book containing the ending they chose to see if their stories are similar to the author's book.

A Good End

| NCTE 1, 2, 3, 4, 5, 6, 11, 12 |

This activity is similar to A Good Beginning. A good ending (last sentence or last paragraph) should resolve the problem, show character growth, and conclude the story in a satisfying way. Common methods for writing endings include narrative description of character (*Old Granny and the Bean Thief* by Cynthia De Felice), narrative summary of problem and resolution (*Bony-Legs* by Joanna Cole), dialogue (*The Wolf's Chicken Stew* by Keiko Kasza), and first person character conclusion (*A Chair for my Mother* by Vera B. Williams). Have students evaluate picture book endings by working with partners to complete the A Good End template (Figure 3.16).

Students will share their findings in small groups. Then they will write their own stories by using one of these techniques for their ending.

Extension

For more work on endings, have students rewrite the story ending they wrote in the A Good End using a different technique. Discuss with them how it changed the story, and which ending is stronger.

And the Ending Is...

| NCTE 1, 2, 3, 4, 5, 6, 11, 12 |

Choose a picture book with a strong plot, such as *Jimmy's Boa and the Bungee Jump Slam Dunk* by Trinka Hakes Noble. Read it aloud to the class, showing the pictures as you read. Read up to the last page of text. Then ask students to write the ending. When everyone is finished, students will read their endings aloud for the class. If you like, have a class vote for best ending and offer prizes. (If you do this, you may like to read the endings aloud yourself or have someone other than the writer read the endings so that the entries are anonymous).

FIGURE 3.16 · A Good End

Name(s) _____

Learn how picture book authors wrote story endings.
Write the book title and put a check mark in the columns that apply to that picture book.

Book Title	Description of Character	Narrative Summary of Problem & Resolution	Dialogue	First Person Character Conclusion	Other (write what)

Summing Up Plot

Sequelizing

NCTE 1, 2, 3, 4, 5, 6, 11, 12   Choose a picture book with a strong plot, such as *Click, Clack, Moo: Cows that Type* by Doreen Cronin. Read it aloud to the class, showing the pictures as you read. When you have finished, ask, "What happened next?" Ask students to write a sequel. They will share their sequels in small groups, with volunteers reading aloud to the entire class.

Summarize

NCTE 1, 2, 3, 4, 5, 6, 11, 12   Plot summaries encourage critical thinking, as students decide what is important and what is not. Explain to students that a plot summary is not a book report, review, or blurb. It is a condensed version of the story. Read aloud a book with a strong plot such as *Lilly's Purple Plastic Purse* by Kevin Henkes. Then ask students to recall the story's main events and record them on the board. Explain that this is the information that goes into a summary.

Read another picture book with a strong plot to the class, such as *Too Many Tamales* by Gary Soto. Then ask students to write summaries of no more than fifty words. They will share their results in small groups. They should listen to ensure that no important part of the story has been omitted.

Transformed Stories

NCTE 1, 2, 3, 4, 5, 6, 11, 12   Have students choose a picture book with a strong plot, such as *The Great Gracie Chase* by Cynthia Rylant or *Where the Wild Things Are* by Maurice Sendak. Wordless picture books also work well here. After they have read it, ask students to write their own versions as poems or songs. Have them share results in small groups, with volunteers presenting their work to the entire class.

Action!

NCTE 1, 2, 3, 4, 5, 6, 11, 12   Working in groups, students will choose a picture book with a strong plot, such as *No, David!* by David Shannon or *Iktomi and the Boulder* by Paul Goble. Ask them to write the story as a script to be acted out or read as a choral reading. Have groups perform their play for the class, a younger grade, parent night, or other special event.

Wordless to Words

NCTE 1, 3, 4, 5, 6, 11, 12 Have wordless books available. Students will choose one and write words for the story based on pictures. Have students read their finished stories aloud to the class, showing the pictures as they read. They may also post their stories to the school Web site, or email or mail their stories to the book's illustrator.

Transitions

Transitions are important in plot, as they help the story flow smoothly from one scene to the next. For more on transitions, see Chapter Two: Setting.

Transition Switch

NCTE 1, 2, 3, 5, 6, 7, 11, 12 Choose a picture book with a strong plot, such as *If You Take a Mouse to School* by Laura Numeroff. Read it aloud to the class, asking them to raise their hands when they hear a transitional word, phrase, or sentence. Read the next sentence to show what the transition is connecting. Then ask students how the meaning of the story would change if a different transition word were used. For example, "How would the meaning of the story change if the transition were "later?" "And?" "Then?"

Students will choose a picture book with a strong plot and rewrite it changing the transitional words, phrases, and sentences. They will share their stories aloud in small groups. When everyone is finished, ask students how their changes altered the story.

Transition Time

NCTE 3, 4, 5, 6, 11, 12 Allow students to do the preparation work for this lesson. Have students type beginnings, middles, and endings of several stories on separate pieces of paper or write them on index cards. Make as many of each category as there are students in class. Put the beginnings in a container labeled "Beginnings," the middles in a container labeled "Middles," and endings in a container labeled "Endings." Ask students to draw one of each. Have them write a story based on their selections, adding transitions between the parts to make the story a whole. Students will read their work aloud in small groups or to the entire class. The class should be able to answer whether the transitions used were effective.

Picture Books with Strong Plots

Aardema, Verna. *Borreguita and the Coyote*, New York: Random, Reprinted ed., 1998. A retold Mexican folktale, where the lamb outwits a coyote to save its life.

Briggs, Raymond. *The Snowman*, New York: Random, 1978. A boy's snowman comes to life and takes the boy flying.

Browne, Anthony. *The Piggybook*, New York: Knopf, 1990. Until Mrs. Piggott leaves home, her family does not appreciate her.

Bunting, Eve. *Fly Away Home*, New York: Clarion, Reissue ed., 1993. A homeless father and son dream of having a home. Meanwhile, they live in an airport.

Carmi, Giora. *A Circle of Friends*, New York: Star Bright, 2003. A boy shares his snack with a homeless man, who shares with the birds. The sharing continues, ending with the boy as receiver.

Cole, Joanna, *Bony-Legs*, New York: Scholastic, Reissue ed., 1980. Based on the Russian Baba Yaga stories. A girl escapes the witch because the witch's dog and cat give her magical items to use.

Cronin, Doreen. *Click, Clack, Moo: Cows that Type*. New York: Simon, 2000. The farmer's cows find a typewriter and use it to make demands. When the demands are not met, they go on strike.

Day, Alexander. *Carl Goes Shopping*, New York: Farrar, 1989. The "Carl" books all follow the same formula, but are delightful in their detail. Carl, a big, black dog, is given instructions to take care of the baby while the baby's mother is busy. Instead, Carl takes the baby on adventures, returning to mother just before she notices they were gone.

_____. *Carl's Afternoon in the Park*, New York: Farrar, 1991.

_____. *Carl's Birthday*, New York: Farrar, 1995.

_____. *Carl's Masquerade*, New York: Farrar, 1993.

_____. *Follow Carl!*, New York: Farrar, 1998.

De Felice, Cynthia. *Old Granny and the Bean Thief*, New York: Farrar, 2003. Old Granny's beans are being stolen. She receives some unusual help in solving the crime.

DePaola, Tomie. *Strega Nona*, New York: Aladdin, 1979. Strega Nona, an Italian witch, has a magic pasta pot. When Big Anthony, Strega Nona's helper, learns the spell, he cannot stop it!

Diakite, Baba Wague. *The Hatseller and the Monkeys,* New York: Scholastic, 1999. A retold West African folktale about a man who goes to market to sell his hats, but has them stolen by monkeys.

Doner, Kim. *Buffalo Dreams*, Portland, OR: Westwinds, 1999. A Native American family travels to see a newly born white buffalo. The girl has a special experience with the animal.

Everitt, Betsy. *Mean Soup,* San Diego: Voyager, 1992. Horace's mother helps him process his anger by showing him how to make Mean Soup.

Felix, Monique. *The Alphabet*, Mankato, MN: Creative Editions, Reissue ed., 1994. A mouse discovers letters of the alphabet.

Fleischman, Paul, *Weslandia,* Cambridge, MA: Candlewick, 1999. Feeling that he does not fit in, Wesley creates his own land and becomes self-sufficient. His classmates are drawn to his new world.

Goble, Paul. *Iktomi and the Boulder*, New York: Orchard, 1988. A retold Plains Indians story. Iktomi, a trickster, lets his arrogance get him into trouble with a boulder.

Haley, Gail E. *A Story! A Story!* Glenview, IL: Foresman, Reprint ed., 1988. A retold African tale that tells how Spider stories came to be.

Hazen, Barbara. *Tight Times*, New York: Puffin, Reprint ed., 1983. A boy who longs for a dog is told by his parents that he cannot have a pet because it is "tight times."

Henkes, Kevin. *Lilly's Purple Plastic Purse,* New York: Greenwillow, 1996. Lilly is so proud of her purse that she disobeys her beloved teacher and plays with it during class. He takes her purse and puts a kind note inside, but Lilly writes her own mean note to the teacher. Lilly learns how to apologize and reconcile.

_____. *Owen*, New York: Greenwillow, 1993. Owen and his parents find a way for him to give up his blanket and keep it at the same time.

Hest, Amy. *When Jessie Came Across the Sea*, Cambridge, MA: Candlewick, 1997. A young Jewish girl leaves her grandmother and comes to the United States, where she works to earn money to bring her grandmother to the United States, too.

Howard, Arthur. *Serious Trouble*, New York: Harcourt, 2003. Prince Ernest's parents are very serious and practical. They disagree with his ambition to be a jester, but he uses his jesting skills to best a dragon.

Hutchins, Pat. *Changes, Changes*, Topeka, KS: Bt Bound, 1999. Two wooden dolls build various structures and shapes from wooden blocks.

Johnston, Tony. *Alice Nizzy Nazzy: The Witch of Santa Fe*, New York: Putnam, 1995. A Southwest version of the traditional Russian Baba Yaga story, where a young girl outsmarts a witch, New Mexico style.

Joyce, William. *Santa Calls*, New York: HarperCollins, 1993. Art Aimesworth's sister gets the Christmas gift she requested from Santa, and Art, his sister, and their friend get an amazing trip to the North Pole.

Kasza, Keiko. *Wolf's Chicken Stew*, New York: Putnam, 1996. The wolf gives treats to the chicken to fatten her up to enhance his stew. When he thinks she should be fat enough, he discovers she has shared the treats with her many children, who are so grateful to "Uncle Wolf," he can't eat them.

Keats, Ezra Jack. *Goggles*, New York: Puffin, Reprint ed., 1978. Henry finds a pair of motorcycle goggles in the trash and fends off bullies so he can keep them.

Kimmel, Eric A. *Hershel and the Hanukkah Goblins*, New York: Holiday House, 1989. Hershel outsmarts the goblins that haunt the synagogue and prevent the people from celebrating Hanukkah.

Kvasnosky, Laura McGee. *Zelda and Ivy*, Cambridge, MA: Candlewick, 1998. A bossy big sister fox and innocent little sister fox learn to love, share, and understand the privileges and pitfalls of birth order.

Lester, Julius. *John Henry*, New York: Dial, 1994. Retelling of the legendary black man who worked hard and tried to cut through a mountain faster than a steam drill.

Lionni, Leo. *Swimmy*, New York: Knopf, 1963. Swimmy, the little black fish, finds a way to fit in and save a school of red fish.

Mayer, Mercer. *A Boy, A Dog, and a Frog*, New York: Dial, 2003. Pictures depict the boy's difficulty in capturing a frog.

_____. *A Boy, A Dog, a Frog, and a Friend,* New York: Dial, 2003. Boy, dog, and frog go fishing, and catch a new friend instead.

_____. *Frog Goes to Dinner*, Topeka, KS: Bt Bound, 1999. Frog jumps from the pocket in which he hid and disrupts dinner in a fancy restaurant.

_____. *Frog on his Own*, Topeka, KS: Bt Bound, 1999. Frog goes to the park with friends, but then goes exploring on his own.

_____. *Frog, Where Are You?*, Topeka, KS: Bt Bound, 1999. Frog escapes and boy and dog go in search of him.

_____. *Liza Lou and the Yeller Belly Swamp*, Topeka, KS: Bt Bound, 1999. Liza Lou outsmarts all the monsters of the Yeller Belly Swamp.

McCully, Emily Arnold. *Mirette on the High Wire*, New York: Putnam, 1992. Set in 1800's Paris, Mirette asks the "Great Bellini" to teach her to walk a tightrope. Bellini faces his fear and reaches his own mastery as Mirette achieves her dream.

McKissack, Patricia. *Flossie and the Fox*, New York: Dutton, 1986. Flossie refuses to be afraid of the fox unless he can prove who he is. In the end, she out-foxes the fox.

Meddaugh, Susan. *Hog-Eye*, Boston: Houghton, Reprint ed., 1998. A pig outsmarts a wolf to save her life.

Ness, Evaline. *Sam, Bangs and Moonshine*, New York: Holt, 1971. Sam, a fisherman's dreamy daughter, learns to distinguish between reality and make-believe.

Noble, Trinka Hakes. *Jimmy's Boa and the Bungee Jump Slam Dunk*, New York: Dial, 2003. Jimmy's boa joins gym class, causing an uproar.

Numeroff, Laura. *If You Take a Mouse to School*, New York: HarperCollins, 2002. If you take a mouse to school, all kinds of things will happen!

Rohmann, Eric. *Time Flies*, New York: Crown, 1994. A bird flies through a museum dinosaur exhibit which becomes real.

Rylant, Cythnia. *The Great Gracie Chase*, New York: Blue Sky, 2001. Gracie, the dog, liked things to be calm and quiet. She preferred the indoors. But when painters come and disrupt her peace, Gracie takes off out the door.

San Souci, Robert D. *The Faithful Friend*, New York: Simon, 1995. Set in the island of Martinique, this is a retelling of a traditional French West Indies tale. Two friends conquer danger and zombies together.

Seeger, Pete. *Abiyoyo*, New York: Simon, Book and CD ed., 2001. The town banishes a father and son, but welcomes them back when they get rid of the giant Abiyoyo.

Sendak, Maurice. *Where the Wild Things Are*, New York: Harper, 1988. Naughty Max is sent to bed without his supper. He dreams of a land where he is king of all the wild things.

Seuss, Dr. *The Cat in the Hat*, New York: Random, 1957. Brother and sister are bored at home alone until the Cat in the Hat shows them how to have his kind of fun.

_____. *How the Grinch Stole Christmas*, New York: Random, 1957. The Grinch tries to steal Christmas from Whoville, but learns that Christmas is not about things.

Shannon, David. *David Goes to School*, New York: Blue Sky Press, 1999. David hears the familiar, "No, David" following his misbehavior at school.

_____. *No, David!*, New York: Scholastic, 1998. David finally gets a hug after doing everything wrong.

Shannon, George. *Dance Away*, Topeka, KS: Bt Bound, 1999. Rabbit dances everywhere, all the time, until his friends are tired of it. They change their minds when Rabbit's dancing saves them from the fox.

Snyder, Dianne. *The Boy of the Three Year Nap*, Boston: Houghton, 1988. A retelling of a traditional Japanese tale, Taro learns the hard way that laziness does not pay.

Soto, Gary. *Too Many Tamales*, New York: Putnam, 1993. Mother and daughters gather to make tamales for the Christmas Eve feast. Maria puts on her mother's wedding ring and loses it. She thinks it is in the tamale dough. Her cousins help look for the ring by eating tamales, only to find the truth.

Steig, William. *Dr. De Soto*, New York: Farrar, 1982. Dentist Dr. De Soto and his wife, both mice, want to help anyone with toothaches. They conceive an ingenious plan to outsmart one of their patients, a fox looking for an easy lunch.

_____. *Sylvester and the Magic Pebble*, New York: Foresman, Reissue ed., 1988. Sylvester the donkey finds a pebble that makes his wishes happen. When a lion frightens him, he wishes to become a rock. Unable to touch the pebble, he remains a rock for a long time. He misses his parents and they miss him. When he is restored and they are reunited, they realize that they have everything they need without wishing for more.

Stevens, Janet. *Coyote Steals the Blanket*, New York: Holiday, 1993. A retelling of a traditional Ute tale, trickster Coyote steals a blanket, angering the desert spirit.

_____. *Tops and Bottoms*, New York: Harcourt, 1995. Based on traditional tales, hare and bear make a deal about farming. Hare outsmarts the lazy bear every time.

Trivizas, Eugene. *The Three Little Wolves and the Big Bad Pig,* New York: McElderry, 1993. A twist on the traditional "Three Little Pigs," this time the pig is after the wolves. The wolves build various types of houses and finally find a way to tame the pig.

Turkle, Brinton. *Do Not Open*, Topeka, KS: Bt Bound, 1999. Miss Moody ignores the warning on a bottle she finds and opens it, unleashing a genie. Wishes do not always turn out the way we expect!

Van Allsburg, Chris. *Jumanji*. Boston: Houghton, 1981. Two children find a board game in the park. They take it home, and when they begin to play, it becomes real, bringing monkeys, a lion, and other dangerous creatures into their home.

Wiesner, David. *Tuesday*, New York: Clarion Books; 1991. A few introductory words lead to the wordless story of frogs flying on lily pads and zooming through neighborhoods while people sleep.

Wells, Rosemary. *Bunny Cakes*, New York: Puffin, 2000. Max and Ruby, bunny siblings, make two special cakes for Grandmas' birthday.

_____. *Yoko*, New York: Hyperion, 1998. Yoko's classmates make fun of her sushi lunch until the class has International Day and they try different foods.

Williams, Vera B. *A Chair for my Mother*, New York: Greenwillow, 1982. A young daughter, grandmother, and waitress mother save money to buy a new chair after they lose their things in a fire.

Wisniewski, David. *Golem*, New York: Clarion, 1996. A Jewish legend, a rabbi brings to life a clay giant to watch over his city of Prague.

Woodruff, Elvira. *The Memory Coat*, New York: Scholastic 1999. A ragged coat is all Grisha has left of his mother. He travels with his cousin Rachel's family to the United States after Jews were attacked in Russia. Going through Ellis Island, Grisha's coat is marked because he has a scratch on his eye. Rachel turns the coat inside-out so the family could enter the United States together.

Young, Ed. *Lon Po Po: A Red-Riding Hood Story from China*, New York: Philomel, 1989. Three sisters who are home alone are tricked into thinking visiting wolf is their grandmother, until they outsmart him.

Zelinsky, Paul O. *Rapunzel*, New York: Dutton, 1997. A retelling of the traditional tale of the girl with long hair locked in a tower.

Zemach, Margaret. *It Could Always Be Worse: A Yiddish Tale*, New York: Simon, 1990. A man with domestic woes seeks help from his rabbi. The man follows the rabbi's advice, adding more people and animals to his household, then taking them out. The story ends with the man in the same situation as he began, only feeling much better about it.

CHAPTER 4

Theme

Big idea, meaning, message, lesson, moral, topic, subject are terms often used interchangeably with "theme." For literary purposes, theme may be defined as the author's usually unstated insight about life. A theme is an exploration of a universal topic, such as love, family, or friendship. In this way, theme is the big idea. Themes can be interpreted and written in statements, but are usually more general than morals or lessons. Themes usually cannot be as fully expressed in an aphorism as a moral can. Theme contributes to good literature's timelessness. One book often has more than one theme.

Definitions and Differentiations

NCTE 1, 3, 6, 11, 12

Theme is a difficult concept to teach, because students are still developing abstract and symbolic thinking (Heffner).

On the board, white board, or overhead transparency, make a chart with these headings: "Plot," "Theme," "Subject," "Moral." Read a book with a strong theme, such as *Five Little Fiends* by Sarah Dyer. Since students should be familiar with plot, begin by asking students what the plot of the story is and write it in the "Plot" column on the chart. ("The five little fiends each take a piece of creation that they have admired for its beauty. In captivity, the pieces are not as beautiful, so the fiends return them.")

Subject is the overt topic of the book. Ask students what the book is about and record their responses in the "Subject" column of the chart. (Responses may include "Sharing," "Ecology," "Stealing," or "Cooperation.")

Students may be familiar with determining the message or moral of a story. If not, define "moral" as the lesson to be learned. Write student responses in the "Moral" column. (Responses could include "You end up with more if you share," or "You can't own nature.")

Theme is related to the responses in the other columns of the chart, but is a bigger, unstated idea. Ask for student responses, but do not write them in the chart yet. You will probably need to hone responses to write a true theme statement or theme statements, which are usually general and not didactic. You may need to ask leading questions, such as "What kind of relationships do you see here?" "Why did the stolen pieces lose their beauty?" When you have a well-polished statement, write it in the chart. (Examples of theme statements are "All the parts of the universe are interconnected" and "True satisfaction comes from sharing."

You may not wish for students to use statements at all, preferring a more general phrase ("the interconnectedness of the universe" and "the satisfaction of sharing" are examples). This method may help students better understand the difference between moral and theme.

Extension

Have the library media specialist show students the value of reading a book's bibliographic record, explaining the record's elements by projecting the image, distributing copies, or using a computer lab setting where each student can look at the online catalog. The bibliographic record shows the author, title, publishing information, local location and availability, edition, and physical description of the book. The bibliographic record often contains an annotation of plot and a list of appropriate Library of Congress Subject Headings, both of which could hint at theme.

From Moral to Theme

NCTE 1, 2, 3, 5, 6, 11, 12 This activity reinforces the difference between morals and themes. Use an edition of *Aesop's Fables,* Ed Young's *Seven Blind Mice,* Arnold Lobel's *Fables* or other picture books with morals at the end. Read one to the class. Ask them to predict the moral, and then read the moral. For example, Lobel's fable "The Crocodile in the Bedroom" contains the moral, "Without a doubt, there is such a thing as too much order." Discuss the truth of the moral. Ask how the moral applies to the story and to contemporary life. Then ask, "What is the theme of this story?" ("What universal truth is explored?") Responses should be similar to the moral, but more general. (The theme of "The Crocodile in the Bedroom" might be "The importance of trying new things" or "Experiencing life is not orderly.") Discuss how an author would rewrite the story to draw out the theme. (The story would not state the moral, for one thing. It may require more character and plot development.)

Have students work individually or with partners to choose a picture book or story containing a moral. They will determine the theme of the story and rewrite the story to draw out the theme, omitting the moral. Students will read the fable and their more thematic stories to the class.

Theme Building

NCTE 1, 2, 3, 4, 5, 6, 11, 12 Themes do not magically appear in books. Authors carefully plan how to build a theme and write their stories to make their desired themes become clear. Have sets of toy blocks available. Students will use them to "build evidence." Read a picture book with a strong theme to the class, such as *Amazing Grace* by Mary Hoffman. Determine one theme ("the power of encouragement," "the importance of believing in oneself," and "race and gender do not hamper dreams and ambitions" are possibilities).

Then study the book, page by page, asking students to find evidence that demonstrates the theme. The student who finds the first one may pick up a block and begin the theme building. Other students will contribute as they volunteer their finds. ("Grace is a good actress, which gives her confidence" is one example). Continue to the end of the book and see what kind of "theme" students have constructed.

Ask students to choose a theme and write a story using that theme. They should include building blocks in plot and character to build their themes. They may use a story they have written previously and revise it to emphasize theme or write a new story.

When everyone has finished their stories, ask students to exchange papers. Distribute the Building Blocks of Theme template (Figure 4.1) and ask students to complete it. Then students should return papers to the stories' authors and answer any questions they have about their classmates' comments.

Layer Cake

NCTE 1, 3, 4, 6, 11, 12 The best books can be understood and enjoyed on several levels. Considering the layers of a book adds to students' greater understanding and appreciation of the story. Make a transparency of the Layer Cake template (Figure 4.2) and project it using an overhead projector. Tell students that you are going to bake a picture book layer cake. Read aloud a picture book with a strong theme, such as *My Friend Rabbit* by Eric Rohmann. Ask students, "What is the plot?" (Sample plot summary: "Rabbit gets into trouble losing a toy airplane in a tree. He pushes other animals into helping him form a pyramid to reach the toy, but the animals fall and become angry. Rabbit's friend, Mouse, is still his friend anyway.") Write their answers in the bottom layer of the cake. This is the basic level of understanding.

Next, ask, "What is the subject?" Students may look at the bibliographic information at the front of the book if they need clues. (Appropriate answers include "Friendship," "Getting into trouble," and "Helping.") Write these answers in the middle layer of the cake on the Layer Cake Template.

Finally, ask, "What is the theme?" If students have difficulty answering, restate the question as "What universal topic is explored?" ("The forgiving nature of friendship," "Loyalty of true friends," "Helping friends in trouble" are some ideas.) Write answers on the top layer of the Layer Cake template.

Distribute Layer Cake templates (Figure 4.2) to students, who will work individually or with partners. They will choose a picture book with a strong theme and complete the template. They will present their results to the class and display their templates in the classroom.

If policy allows, bring in a layer cake to eat in celebration of this activity.

FIGURE 4.1 # Building Blocks of Theme

Name(s) _____   Date _____

Did the author of the story successfully build a theme? Read the story and complete the blanks below. Then re-read the story to find the theme's building blocks. Write them in the blocks below. You might not need to use every block.

Author's Name _____

Theme _____

FIGURE 4.2 # Layer Cake

Name(s) _____   Date _____

Picture Book Title _____

Theme _____

Good stories have several layers, just like a layer cake. Choose a picture book and complete the template, making the bottom layer first, the middle layer second, and the top layer third. Present your cake to the class when you have finished.

Write story theme here.

Write story subject here.

Write story plot summary here.

Extensions

- Ask students to imagine a story with a similar plot, but different theme. Have them write that story. Share results with small groups or the class.

- Ask students to write a story about the same subject, but different plot. Share results with small groups or the class.

Theme Supreme

NCTE 1, 2, 3, 4, 5, 6, 11, 12   When students have had practice with themes, ask them to work individually and choose a picture book with a strong theme. Distribute the Theme Supreme template (Figure 4.3) or provide a word processing document to help students articulate theme and write stories. Using strategies they have learned, they will each determine their book's theme. Then have students write or type their own stories with the same or similar themes. Share results aloud with small groups or whole class. Discuss differences between student stories and the correlating picture books. Ask students to notice story differences and similarities among those students who used similar themes.

Extension

Working individually, students will choose a picture book with a strong theme, identify the theme, and write a story with an opposing theme. For example, if the theme is determined to be "the joy of friendship," the student will write a story with the theme, "the trials and tribulations of friendship."

To Agree or Disagree

NCTE 1, 3, 4, 5, 6, 11, 12   Explain to students that authors usually express their own views and feelings in their books' themes. Choose a book with a strong theme, such as *The Table Where the Rich People Sit* by Byrd Baylor. Read the book aloud to the class, determine the theme or themes, and record responses on the board, white board, overhead transparency, or flip chart. Ask students whether they agree with the author's view of the theme and why or why not. Have students write essays explaining their positions, sharing the results in small groups.

Variation

After guided practice activity, ask students to work individually to choose picture books with strong themes. Have them determine the theme and decide why they agree or disagree with the author's view of theme. They will write essays explaining their positions, sharing results in small groups or turning their essays in for a grade.

FIGURE 4.3 **Theme Supreme**

Name(s) _____ Date _____

Picture Book Title _____

Theme _____

Write your own story with the same or similar theme in the space below. Use the back of the page and extra paper if necessary.

_____

_____

_____

_____

_____

_____

_____

_____

_____

_____

_____

_____

_____

_____

_____

_____

_____

_____

_____

_____

_____

This is block style:

Sender's name and address (three or four lines)

Space

Date

Space

Recipient's name and address (three or four lines)

Space

Salutation

Space

Body of the letter

Space

Closing

Four spaces

Sender's name

Tell Them About It

NCTE 1, 3, 4, 5, 6, 11, 12 Working with partners, have students will choose a picture book with a strong theme and identify its theme. (Books with social and political themes, such *Fly Away Home* by Eve Bunting, work best for this activity.) Ask them to write a letter to the editor of a newspaper or a letter to an elected official telling why you agree or disagree with the theme. In the letter, students should tell what they want done. (Ask, "What do you think the community should do?" and, "What do you think your elected official should do?" to help students complete the assignment.)

Teach proper business letter format as shown and assign students to use it.

Students may also use the business letter template in a computer word processing program. The library media specialist can help students find correct mailing addresses for recipients and correct forms of address for the salutations. Students will turn in their letters. If some themes and letters are appropriate, obtain students' permission to mail them. Ask them to share with the class any responses they receive.

Variation

Rather than write a business letter, ask students to write essays persuading others to accept their opinions about a certain book's theme.

Slogans, Billboards, Themes

NCTE 1, 3, 4, 5, 6, 8, 11, 12 Working in small groups, have students read at least three picture books and identify themes. Each group will select one theme and design an advertising campaign related to the theme. You may invite an advertising representative to speak to the class about the components of an ad campaign. Such a campaign can include radio, TV, Internet, and newspaper ads; brochures; billboards; products to give away, and contests. Allow two weeks for groups to develop their campaigns. They may use standard art supplies, computer graphics software, word processing software, audio equipment, or any media to convey their message. When all have completed their projects, the groups will present their campaigns to the class.

Stir the Story Pot

NCTE 1, 3, 4, 5, 6, 11, 12 Set a cooking pot with a lid in the classroom or library. Label the pot "Story Pot." Ask students to read at least three picture books with strong themes. They will determine themes, write each theme and the title of the book they read on a piece of paper, and put the papers in the Story Pot.

When all students have submitted their themes, announce, "It is time to stir the Story Pot." Stir the pot with a spoon or by hand. Have each student select one piece of paper from the Story Pot and write a story containing the theme he or she selected. Share completed stories in small groups or with the class. Ask students to determine each story's theme. Does it match the theme the author selected? Why or why not? If not, how could the story be changed so that it does match the theme?

See the Theme

NCTE 1, 3, 4, 5, 6, 8, 11, 12 Working individually or in small groups, students read at least three picture books with strong themes. They will identify themes and choose one. Collaborate with the art teacher or technology teacher to assist with the art project. Using standard art supplies, computer graphics software, or computer word processing software, students will create a poster or collage representing the chosen theme. It should include words and phrases from the selected picture book. Have students present their creations to the class, explaining theme and its representations. Art should be displayed in the classroom, library, or somewhere for the whole school to enjoy.

Picture Books with Strong Themes

Aesop's Fables. Many editions available. One is illustrated by Jerry Pinkney, New York: SeaStar, 2000. Traditional tales ending with morals, meant to teach a lesson.

Altman, Linda Jacobs. *The Legend of Freedom Hill*, New York: Lee, 2000. Set during the California Gold Rush, black Rosabel and Jewish Sophie work together to buy Rosabel's mother freedom from slavery.

Andersen, Hans Christian. Jerry Pinkney, il. *Ugly Duckling*, New York: Morrow, 1999. A version of the traditional story of an ugly duckling turning into a beautiful swan.

Andreae, Giles. *Giraffes Can't Dance*, New York: Orchard, 2001. Gerald the giraffe is a laughingstock because he can't dance the way other animals do. Then he finds his own way to dance.

Baylor, Byrd. *Everybody Needs a Rock*, Glenview, IL: Foresman, 1974. What makes a rock perfect? What can you do with a rock? Why do you need a rock?

_____. *The Table Where the Rich People Sit*, New York: Atheneum, 1994. A child is angry with her family for being poor, but talking at a family meeting reveals just how rich the family is.

Brown, Marcia. *Once a Mouse....*, New York: Scribner, 1961. A traditional tale from India. A mouse becomes a cat, which becomes a dog, and continues to change everything but attitude.

Brown, Margaret Wise. *The Runaway Bunny*, New York: Harper, 1972, 1942. A bunny runs away from home, but is always safe because his mother is right behind him.

Bunting, Eve. *Fly Away Home*, New York: Clarion, 1989. A homeless father and son dream of having a home. Meanwhile, they live in an airport.

_____. *Smoky Night*, New York: Harcourt, 1994. The Los Angeles riots ripped neighborhoods apart, but this story tells about a boy and his family who learn how to come together with people who are different.

_____. *The Wednesday Surprise*, New York: Clarion, 1989. The family thinks Grandma is teaching Anna to read. Imagine their surprise when they learn it is Anna who is teaching Grandma to read.

Buscaglia, Leo. *The Fall of Freddie the Leaf,* New York: Holt, 20th anniversary ed., 2002. Freddie and his leaf friends learn about the cycle of life and death.

Cannon, Janell. *Stellaluna*, New York: Harcourt, 1993. Stellaluna, a young bat, is separated from her mother and raised by birds. Stellaluna takes on birds' ways, even though she finds them odd. She is later reunited with her mother, who teaches her bat ways again. Stellaluna learns how to be friends with those who are different without sacrificing her own ways.

Carmi, Giora. *A Circle of Friends*, New York: Star Bright, 2003. A boy shares his snack with a homeless man, who shares with the birds. The sharing continues, ending with the boy as receiver.

Casler, Leigh. *The Boy Who Dreamed of an Acorn*. New York: Philomel, 1994. A young boy of the Chinook Indian tribe goes on a vision quest and learns what his dream of an acorn has to do with his place in the tribe.

Clifton, Lucille. *Everett Anderson's Friend*. New York: Holt, 1992. Young Everett is disappointed to find that his new neighbor children are all girls, but learns they can be friends anyway.

Cooney, Barbara. *Chanticleer and the Fox*. Springfield, OH: Crowell, 1958. Based on Chaucer's "Nun's Priest's Tale," a fox uses flattery to try to outsmart a rooster.

Coursen, Valerie. *Mordant's Wish*, New York: Holt, 1997. Mordant the mole wishes that a turtle-shaped cloud could turn into a real turtle friend. It becomes reality, and Mordant's wishing continues.

Cutler, Jane. *The Cello of Mr. O*, New York: Dutton, 1999. Mr. O plays his cello in the middle of the community, distracting the war- and-poverty-stricken children from their hunger during an unnamed war in modern times.

Demi. *The Empty Pot*, New York: Holt, 1990. A Chinese folktale. Ping's honesty is rewarded when he admits that he cannot grow a flower from the Emperor's seeds.

De Paola, Tomie. *Nana Upstairs & Nana Downstairs*. New York: Puffin, Reissue ed., 2000. A young boy learns about death in loving his grandmother and ill great-grandmother.

_____. *Oliver Button is a Sissy*, New York: Harcourt, 1979. Oliver is not a jock. He prefers dancing, painting, and reading. For this he is tormented by his classmates, but is undeterred in following his pursuits.

Dyer, Sarah. *Five Little Fiends*, New York: Dutton, 2001. Five little fiends love parts of the world so much that they take them for their own. They soon realize the world was more beautiful when all the elements were together.

Eduar, Gilles. *Jooka Saves the Day*, New York: Orchard, 1997. A wise pelican teaches Jooka the "crocodile" (who is really a dragon) that his differences are gifts.

Egan, Tim. *Metropolitan Cow*. Boston: Houghton, 1996. Bennett, the son of urban cows, befriends his new neighbor, Webster the pig, much to the chagrin of Bennett's parents.

Elliott, Laura Malone. *Hunter's Best Friend at School*, New York: HarperCollins, 2002. Hunter and Stripe are best friends. But when Hunter follows Stripe's lead, he gets into trouble at school. Can he behave and remain friends with Stripe?

Ernst, Lisa Campbell. *Zinnia and Dot*, New York: Viking, 1992. Zinnia and Dot are two competitive chickens who put aside their differences to save an egg from a weasel.

Everitt, Betsy. *Mean Soup*, New York: Harcourt, 1992. Horace's mother helps him process his anger by showing him how to make Mean Soup.

Fine, Edith Hope. *Under the Lemon Moon*, New York: Lee, 1999. Someone is stealing Rosalinda's lemons! Not only that, but her lemon tree is sick. She seeks help and offers forgiveness and aide to the thief.

Gackenback, Dick. *Claude the Dog*, New York: Seabury, 1974. Claude the dog is well-loved by his owners and receives many Christmas gifts. When he meets a needier dog, he gives all his gifts away.

Haas, Jesse. *Busybody Brandy*, New York: Greenwillow, 1990. Brandy, the farm dog, seems like a busybody during the day, snooping into all the other animals' business. At night, however, Brandy alerts the animals to a potential threat and is appreciated.

Henkes, Kevin. *Julius, the Baby of the World*, New York: Greenwillow, 1990. Lilly finds her new baby brother disgusting, until she defends him against her cousin.

Hoffman, Mary. *Amazing Grace*, Glenview, IL: Foresman, 1991. In spite of race and gender, Grace proves she can be Peter Pan.

Isadora, Rachel. *Max*, Springfield, OH: Collier, 1984, 1976. Max discovers that ballet dancing helps him warm up for his baseball games.

Jackson, Isaac. *Somebody's New Pajamas*, New York: Dial, 1996. After spending the night at his friend Robert's house, Jerome is embarrassed that his family does not live in such a nice place. Jerome does not even wear pajamas! When Jerome has Robert stay at his house, Robert learns to sleep in his underwear, and both boys realize that friendship is more important than socioeconomic standing.

Johnston, Tony. *Sparky and Eddie: The First Day of School*, New York: Scholastic, 1997. Sparky and Eddie are best friends, but their friendship is tested when they begin school and are assigned to different rooms.

Joose, Barbara. *Mama, Do You Love Me?* San Francisco: Chronicle, 1991. A mother in the Arctic reassures that she loves her child no matter what.

Lester, Helen. *Hooway for Wodney Wat*, Boston: Houghton, 1999. Wodney Wat, much maligned for his speech impediment, uses his handicap to eliminate a bully from his class.

Lewin, Hugh. *Jafta's Father*, Minneapolis: Carolrhoda, 1983, 1981. Set in South Africa. Jafta's father works in the city during the winter. Jafta looks forward to his father's return home in the spring.

Lionni, Leo. *Frederick*, New York: Knopf, 1987. Frederick, the mouse, does not toil like his brothers, but he shares his special talents to help them all last through the winter.

_____. *Swimmy*. New York: Pantheon, 1963. Swimmy, the little black fish, finds a way to fit in and save a school of red fish.

Lipkind, William and Nicolas Mordivinoff. *Finders Keepers*, New York: Harcourt, 1989. Two dogs dig and uncover a bone simultaneously. Who gets to keep it?

Lobel, Arnold. *Fables*, New York: HarperCollins, 1980. Original tales with a moral at the end.

McCourt, Lisa. *I Miss You, Stinky Face*, Mahwah, NJ: Troll, 1999. Even if the child turned into something ugly, the mother would still love the child.

Mitchell, Lori. *Different Just Like Me*, Watertown, MA: Charlesbridge, 1999. April watches people she sees as she rides a bus and concludes that we are all different, but alike, too.

Munsch, Robert. *Love You Forever*, Willowdale, Ontario, CN: Firefly, 1989. Mother and son promise to love each other forever.

Polacco, Patricia. *Pink and Say*, New York: Philomel, 1994. Based on a true story, black Union soldier, Pink, finds injured white soldier Say, takes him home, and, with the help of his mother, nurses Say back to health. They develop a strong friendship. Both are taken to Andersonville where Pink is hanged.

Rathmann, Peggy. *Officer Buckle and Gloria*, New York: Putnam, 1995. Officer Buckle's school safety speeches improve dramatically with the help of his canine partner, Gloria.

Rohmann, Eric. *My Friend Rabbit*, Brookfield, CT: Roaring Brook, 2002. Rabbit has a way of making things go awry, but his friend loves him anyway.

Say, Allen. *Stranger in the Mirror*, Boston: Houghton, 1995. A young boy turns into his grandfather overnight. He fears being taken away, as his grandfather was. Sam is taken to the doctor, who can find nothing wrong. He is taunted at school. He regains himself when he remembers that he is still himself.

Scheffler, Ursel. *Who Has Time for Little Bear?*, New York: Doubleday, 1998. Little Bear's parents are too busy to play with him. Fortunately, he finds another bear in a similar situation, and they become friends.

Shulevitz, Uri. *The Treasure*, New York: Farrar, 1979. Retold English tale. A man follows advice he receives in a dream and eventually finds treasure.

Silverstein, Shel. *The Giving Tree*, New York: HarperCollins, 1964. The tree nurtures the boy until the tree is just an old stump and the boy is an old man.

Van Allsburg, Chris. *The Sweetest Fig*, Boston: Houghton, 1993. Monsieur Bibot is given two magical figs. While he decides what to do with them, his dog intervenes.

Williams, Vera B. *A Chair for my Mother*, New York: Greenwillow, 1983. A young daughter, grandmother, and waitress mother save money to buy a new chair after they lose their things in a fire.

Wood, Douglas. *Old Turtle*, New York: Scholastic, 2001. Old Turtle tries to explain who God is among the arguing animals.

Yorinks, Arthur. *Hey, Al*, New York: Farrar, 1986. A tropical bird lifts a custodian and his dog to an island paradise, where they begin to turn into birds.

Young, Ed. *Seven Blind Mice*, New York: Philomel, 1992. An adaptation of "The Blind Men and the Elephant." In this case, the blind are mice, each determining a different aspect of the elephant.

Zemach, Harve. *The Judge: An Untrue Tale*, New York: Farrar, 1969. The judge puts people in prison, only to find out that they have told the truth.

Zemach, Margot. *It Could Always Be Worse: A Yiddish Tale*, New York: Simon, 1990. A man with domestic woes seeks help from his rabbi. The man follows the rabbi's advice, adding more people and animals to his household, then taking them out. The story ends with the man in the same situation as he began, only feeling much better about it.

CHAPTER

Style 5

Style includes such a variety of nuances that it is difficult to define. Style includes voice, mood, syntax, and diction. Style gives personality and emotion to writing. As individual as snowflakes, it develops over time. Writers with a recognizable style have been in the business awhile, but recognizing other writers' styles is a step toward developing one's own (Thomason, 62). Learning about style encourages students to revise their work and gives them the desire to make a piece truly theirs. It creates awareness of the many decisions authors make when creating a story.

Introduction to Style with Music and Art

NCTE 1, 3, 6, 8, 11, 12 This lesson may take place over several class periods. Make an audiocassette tape or CD with short clips of various styles of classical music. Include Bach, Beethoven, Debussy, and Rachmaninoff. (Use any genre of music, as long as the clips are distinctly different from one another.) Play each clip and ask students to describe it, as you record their answers on the board or on an overhead/transparency. Collaborate with the music teacher to give the class more information about the music and composers. Explain that although all the clips are considered classical music (or music of the same type), they are quite different.

Show students several picture books illustrated by the same person; for example, Jan Brett. Ask students to notice similarities among the illustrations. What makes the illustrations recognizable as the illustrator's? Then show them several picture books illustrated by a different artist who uses a different style; for example,

Peter Parnall. Again, ask students to notice similarities among these illustrations. What makes the illustrations recognizable as the illustrator's? Then compare the work of the two illustrators. Discuss the differences and why each is successful for the type of books they illustrate. Collaborate with the art teacher or direct students to <http://picturingbooks.imaginarylands.org> to give the class more information about illustrations.

While students may prefer one illustrator's style over another, ask them how appropriate the art is for the story it illustrates. Ask how the effect of the picture book would be different if a different style of art were used. For example, *Too Many Tamales* by Gary Soto is a realistically illustrated book. What effect would cartoonish illustrations have on the story?

Many Versions

NCTE 1, 2, 3, 4, 5, 6, 7, 11, 12 This lesson may take place over more than one class period. It is best conducted in the library. Gather several versions of the same story, featuring different illustrators. Fairy tales and folktales work well for this demonstration. Students will work in small groups, with each group studying one version of the story. Distribute the Many Versions template (Figure 5.1), asking groups to complete it. Distribute the Comparing Many Versions template (Figure 5.2) to each student. When all the groups are finished, each group will present their findings and show their book's artwork. As students listen to the presentations, ask them to complete the Comparing Many Versions template.

Ask students to write their own version of the story. They may also illustrate it. They will share their stories in small groups or with the class.

Variation

Gather several sets of various versions of the same story, featuring different illustrators. (For example, several differently illustrated versions of *Rapunzel*, several differently illustrated versions of *Cinderella*, and so on.) Students will work in small groups, with each group studying one story. Distribute the Comparing Many Versions template (Figure 5.2) to each group. When all the groups are finished, each group will present their findings and show their books' artwork. After the presentations, ask what students noticed overall. Which treatments did they think were most successful for the story? If more than one group had a version by the same illustrator, were the illustrations similar? Reinforce the concept of style.

FIGURE 5.1 # Many Versions

Name(s) _____ Date _____

Study the picture book and complete the template. When everyone is finished, each group will present their findings and show their book's artwork.

Our Book Title _____

Our Book Author and Illustrator _____

Plot Summary _____

_____

_____

_____

_____

_____

_____

_____

_____

_____

_____

_____

_____

_____

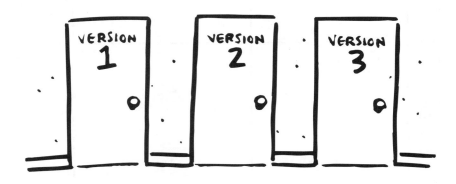

FIGURE 5.2

Comparing Many Versions

Name(s) _____

Book Title	Author	Illustrator	Plot Summary	Art Description

Word Choice Awareness

One element of style in written work is word choice. "Diction" refers to word choice and "syntax" refers to the way words are put together to form phrases or sentences.

Picture books say a lot with a few words, so language must be especially precise. Precise word choice helps the reader envision "convertible" instead of "car." Word choice contributes to the mood, or feeling, of a story. Notice the difference between "The storm swirled around them" and "The weather was windy and rainy." Students gain awareness of diction and syntax by reading and hearing the work of professional authors. Choose several picture books with especially strong syntax and diction and read them aloud to students. Books with strong syntax and diction include:

Owl Moon by Jane Yolen	*The Cat in the Hat* by Dr. Seuss
Smoky Night by Eve Bunting	*Saving Sweetness* by Diane Stanley
Mountain Dance by Thomas Locker	*The Girl Who Loved Wild Horses* by Paul Goble
Jumanji by Chris Van Allsburg	
Pink and Say by Patricia Polacco	*Green Eyes* by Abe Birnbaum
I'm in Charge of Celebrations by Byrd Baylor	*Weslandia* by Paul Fleischman
	My Mama had a Dancing Heart by Libba Moore Gray
Owen by Kevin Henkes	*Tough Cookie* by David Wisniewski

Encourage students to keep a separate notebook or a separate section of a notebook in which they write down words or phrases they like. After hearing a story, have students share with the class or in small groups the words or phrases they chose. Ask them why those words and phrases were so appealing.

Explain to students that while they need to develop their own ways with words, they can learn and practice by using other authors' words. Ask students to take one of the phrases they wrote down in their notebooks and write their own original paragraph or story using that phrase. When everyone is finished, students will share in small groups.

Finding specifics

Explain the difference between general ("day") and specific ("Monday"). Choose a picture book with rich details and read it aloud to the class, asking students to jot specific details they hear in their notebooks. For examples of books with specific details, see the list in the Word Choice Awareness Section. Discuss results.

Working in small groups, students will read up to three picture books with specific details. Distribute the Finding Specifics template (Figure 5.3) and ask students to complete it. When groups are finished, discuss their findings. Ask, "What would the general term for that be?" "What was the effect of that detail?" "Why did the author choose to specify that detail?" "What specifics did you especially like?"

FIGURE 5.3 **Finding Specifics**

Name(s) _____ Date _____

Read one, two, or three picture books. Complete the blanks for title and author below. Write down the specific details you find. Be ready to discuss your results with the class.

1 Title _____

Author _____

Details _____

_____

_____

2 Title _____

Author _____

Details _____

_____

_____

3 Title _____

Author _____

Details _____

_____

_____

From General to Specific

NCTE 3, 4, 5, 6, 11, 12 Successful authors use more specific words than general ones. Details make images stronger and make stories more interesting. Details may also make a difference in story interpretation, such as in the difference between "sandals" and "mukluks." Distribute the From General to Specific template (Figure 5.4) and ask students to complete it. When they have finished, ask them to choose three specifics and write a story or essay using them. They will share results in small groups.

Verb Verve

NCTE 3, 4, 5, 6, 11, 12 To show the necessity of strong verbs, choose a picture book with strong verbs and read it aloud. Books with strong verbs include:

Weslandia by Paul Fleischman	*Iktomi and the Boulder* by Paul Goble
Hooway for Wodney Wat by Helen Lester	*Stellaluna* by Janell Cannon
Lilly's Purple Plastic Purse by Kevin Henkes	*Dr. De Soto* by William Steig

Ask students to listen for strong verbs and write them in their notebooks. After the story, students will share the verbs they wrote down by saying the verbs and acting them out. Discuss why the author might have chosen those verbs.

In small groups, students will choose a verb from their lists. Distribute the Verb Verve template (Figure 5.5). Have them find and copy the sentence where the verb appeared. They will complete the template and share results with the class when all groups are finished.

Figures of Speech Hunt

NCTE 1, 2, 3, 4, 5, 6, 11, 12 The library media specialist and teacher should collaborate for this lesson. The lesson may take more than one class period. Figures of speech add a sense of region, character education and background, and imagery to stories.

Introduce or review the figures of speech listed on page 110. Read a picture book containing figures of speech. (See suggestions listed under Word Choice Awareness on page 105). Ask students to listen for figures of speech and write them down. When you have finished reading, students will share results. Discuss which figures of speech they liked, which they didn't, and whether there were any they did not understand.

Distribute Figures of Speech Hunt template (Figure 5.6). Working in pairs, students will go on a Figures of Speech Hunt in the library, writing down figures of speech they find in picture books, along with title and author. Appropriate authors are given on the template. (Enlist volunteer help to shelve books after the hunt, if necessary). After the hunt, students will work in small groups reading their results. Ask each group to determine their top three favorites to report to the class.

FIGURE 5.4 # From General to Specific

Name(s) _____   Date _____

Read the general term on the left. Think of a specific term and write it in the column on the right. For example, if the general term is "soap," a specific term is "Ivory."

GENERAL	SPECIFIC
Cars	
Cereal	
Fruit	
Candy	
Movies	
Color	
Insects	
Birds	
Sports	
Shoes	

When you are finished, choose three specific words and use them in a story. You will share your story aloud in a small group.

FIGURE 5.5   Verb Verve

Name(s) _____   Date _____

Choose a verb from one of your lists and complete the blank. Find the sentence in the picture book in which it appears and complete the blank.

Verb _____

Sentence in which the verb appears_____

_____

_____

Write down synonyms for the verb. Use a thesaurus if you like.

_____

_____

Now read the sentence aloud, replacing the original verb with synonyms. Why do you think the author chose the verb he or she did? Write your answer here and be prepared to share with the class.

_____

_____

_____

_____

_____

_____

_____

_____

_____

_____

Figures of speech include

Metaphor	A direct comparison; something is something else. "Love is a rose."
Simile	An indirect comparison; something is like something else. "My love is like a red, red rose."
Imagery	Language that appeals to the senses and creates a picture in the mind or feeling in the heart. Often uses metaphor and simile.
Idiom	A dialectic or regional grammatically non-sensical expression. "Outen the light" meaning "turn off the light," for example.
Cliche	Trite, overused expression. "Red as a beet," for example. Should not appear in professional writing unless in dialogue or for some distinct purpose. Avoid in writing.
Slang	Informal, non-standard word or phrase used by a particular group. "Way cool," for example. Should only be used if appropriate to audience or in dialogue.

Have students choose a favorite figure of speech and incorporate it into an original story. They will share their finished stories in small groups or with the class.

Sentenced!

NCTE 1, 3, 4, 5, 6, 11, 12 The flow of a sentence and of a series of sentences affects the mood of the story and also sets the pace of the plot. (See "Pacing" in Chapter 3.) Sentence construction also influences how easy or difficult the text is to read. Teach or review with students the types of sentence construction.

Types of Sentences

Simple	One independent clause. "Janet ran home."
Compound	Two or more independent clauses. "Janet ran home, and Nita ran with her."
Complex	One independent clause and at least one subordinate clause. "When the dog chased them, Janet and Nita ran home."
Compound-Complex	Two or more independent clauses and at least one subordinate clause. "When the dog chased them, Janet and Nita ran home, and they called their mother."

FIGURE 5.6

Figures of Speech Hunt

Name _____

Look for figures of speech in picture books. When you find them, copy them into the appropriate box in the chart. Try to find as many as you can. These authors are especially good at using figures of speech: Jane Yolan, Byrd Baylor, Eve Bunting, Patricia Polacco, William Steig, Cynthia Rylant, Trinka Hakes Noble, and David Wisniewski.

AUTHOR	TITLE	FIGURES OF SPEECH

Choose a picture book such as *Sparky and Eddie: The First Day of School* by Tony Johnston, and read it aloud to the class. Then re-read it aloud. Show the text, if possible, remembering copyright restrictions. Stop reading after each sentence so students can identify the sentence type. The first sentence of *Sparky and Eddie: The First Day of School* is "Sparky and Eddie lived next door to each other," a simple sentence. Continue until you have identified the types of all the sentences.

Look at the story again. This time, ask students how they could combine sentences to create compound or complex sentences. An example from *Sparky and Eddie: The First Day of School* changes sentences on page eight to "Because Sparky was born on the Fourth of July, he was named for sparklers." This turns two simple sentences into a complex sentence. Continue through the book and see what changes students can make. Discuss why the author wrote the story the way he or she did. Guide students toward a recognition of intended audience and their reading ability.

Have students choose a simple picture book and change sentences as in the Sparky and Eddie: The First Day of School model. Other *Sparky and Eddie* books, Cynthia Rylant's *Henry and Mudge* books, and Rosemary Wells' books are appropriate suggestions for this activity. In small groups, students will compare their versions to the originals. They will discuss why the authors used the sentence types they did. Groups will report to the whole class.

Extension

Following Sentenced! repeat the lesson with a more difficult book, such as *Pink and Say* by Patricia Polacco.

In the Mood

NCTE 1, 3, 4, 5, 6, 11, 12

Mood evokes emotion in readers. It connects our hearts to the story. As previously mentioned in this chapter, word choice and sentence type contribute to mood. Mood is also closely connected with voice. In literature, mood can be described as heavy, dark, light, happy, spooky, funny, thoughtful, and powerful, to list a few.

Choose a picture book with an easily definable mood. Examples of books with easily definable mood are:

Owl Moon by Jane Yolen

Smoky Night by Eve Bunting

The Cello of Mr. O by Jane Cutler

Nana Upstairs & Nana Downstairs by Tomie DePaola

Amazing Grace by Mary Hoffman

Mama, Do You Love Me? by Barbara Joose

Pink and Say by Patricia Polacco

When Marian Sang by Pamela Muñoz Ryan

When I Was Young in the Mountains by Cynthia Rylant

Saving Sweetness by Diane Stanley

I'll Fix Anthony by Judith Viorst

The Way to Start A Day by Byrd Baylor

The Man Who Walked Between the Towers by Mordicai Gerstein

The Secret of the North Pole by Arcadio Lobato

The Day Jimmy's Boa Ate the Wash by Trinka Hakes Noble

Click, Clack, Moo: Cows that Type by Doreen Cronin

The Great Gracie Chase by Cynthia Rylant

Jumanji by Chris Van Allsburg

Tough Cookie by David Wisniewski

Read the book aloud to the class, asking them to think about their feelings as you read. When you are finished reading, ask students what feeling the book as a whole gave them. Ask what about the story gave them that feeling and record answers. Then read a book with a different mood and repeat the process. Also ask and note whether the books changed mood from beginning to end.

Ask students to choose one of the moods they identified and write a story that reflects that mood. When they are finished, have them exchange papers. Readers will write the mood they think the story reflects. When papers are returned to the owners, conferencing should cover whether the correct mood was being evoked. If not, how could the writer have been more effective?

Extension

Ask students to use the story they wrote in the previous exercise, but rewrite it so that the mood is different.

Voice

Be Yourself

| NCTE 1, 3, 4, 5, 6, 11, 12 |

Voice is that hard-to-define quality that makes a writer *that* writer, and no one else. It adds personality to a written work. Voice means letting yourself show through in the writing. While the same writer can write in a humorous, serious, sarcastic, thoughtful, or angry tone, some unique trait identifies that writer. Two writers could write about the same thing with completely different results. No one has exactly the same memories, experiences, or imaginations.

Read a picture book, discuss the author's voice, and then assign students to write about the same topic. For example, read *The Cafeteria Lady from the Black Lagoon* by Mike Thaler or another story about school cafeterias. Ask students to write about the school cafeteria, allowing their voices to show in their work. When everyone is finished, work in small groups reading each other's papers. Try to identify mood and voice. When the groups have finished, discuss as a class similarities and differences in the papers. Ask students to especially consider their classmate's word choice, mood, and theme.

Identifying Voice

| NCTE 1, 2, 3, 4, 5, 6, 7, 11, 12 |

Help students better understand voice by having them study several books by the same author. Have students work in groups, with each group reading picture books by one author. Suggested authors are Eve Bunting, Rosemary Wells, Dr. Seuss, Byrd Baylor, William Steig, Patricia Polacco, Chris Van Allsburg, Kevin Henkes, and Tomie DePaola. Distribute the Identifying Voice template (Figure 5.7), and ask students to complete it. When groups are finished, they will report to the class.

Extension

The library media specialist can help students do critical research on their author, showing them reference material, professional criticism of the author's books, and pertinent Web sites.

FIGURE 5.7 # Identifying Voice

Name(s) _____   Date _____

Complete the blanks and be prepared to present your findings to the class.

Our author is _____

The books we read were _____

_____

_____

What we noticed about word choice (give examples from the books) _____

_____

_____

_____

What we noticed about mood (give examples from the books) _____

_____

_____

_____

What we noticed about themes (give examples from the books) _____

_____

_____

_____

What makes this author unique?_____

_____

_____

_____

Picture Books Used to Discuss Style

Baylor, Byrd. *I'm in Charge of Celebrations,* New York: Atheneum, 1986. Describes celebrating everyday life in the desert.

_____. *The Way to Start A Day,* New York: Atheneum, 1978. Describes how people around the world greet the new day.

_____. Various others.

Brett, Jan. Various.

Birnbaum, Abe. *Green Eyes*, New York: Golden, Deluxe ed., 2001. A white cat with green eyes tells about its first year of life.

Bunting, Eve. *Smoky Night,* New York: Harcourt, 1994. The Los Angeles riots ripped neighborhoods apart, but this story tells about a boy and his family who learn how to come together with people who are different.

_____. Various others.

Cannon, Janell. *Stellaluna*, New York: Harcourt, 1993. Stellaluna, a young bat, is separated from her mother and raised by birds. Stellaluna takes on birds' ways, even though she finds them odd. She is later reunited with her mother, who teaches her bat ways again. Stellaluna learns how to be friends with those who are different without sacrificing her own ways.

Cinderella. Various eds.

Cronin, Doreen. *Click, Clack, Moo: Cows that Type,* New York: Simon, 2000. The farmer's cows find a typewriter and use it to make demands. When the demands are not met, they go on strike.

Cutler, Jane. *The Cello of Mr. O*, New York: Dutton, 1999. Mr. O plays his cello in the middle of the community, distracting the war- and-poverty-stricken children from their hunger during an unnamed war in modern times.

DePaola, Tomie. *Nana Upstairs & Nana Downstairs,* New York: Puffin, Reissue ed., 2000. A young boy learns about death in loving his grandmother and ill great-grandmother.

_____. Various others.

Fleischman, Paul. *Weslandia*, Cambridge, MA: Candlewick, 1999. Feeling that he does not fit in, Wesley creates his own land and becomes self-sufficient. His classmates are drawn to his new world.

Gerstein, Mordicai. *The Man Who Walked Between the Towers*, Brookfield, CT: Millbrook, 2003. In 1974, Philippe Petit walked on a high wire between the World Trade Center towers. This book commemorates the event, citing Petit's skill and courage, and paying tribute to the great towers.

Goble, Paul. *The Girl Who Loved Wild Horses,* Glenview, IL: Foresman, Reissue ed., 1993. A retold Native American tale. A girl loves her people, but loves the wild horses more. Her village releases her to them, and they run away together.

_____. *Iktomi and the Boulder,* New York: Orchard, 1988. A retold Plains Indians story. Iktomi, a trickster, lets his arrogance get him into trouble with a boulder.

Gray, Libba Moore. *My Mama had a Dancing Heart,* New York: Orchard, 1995. Mama danced and celebrated each new season, inspiring her daughter, who is now a ballet dancer.

Henkes, Kevin. *Lilly's Purple Plastic Purse,* New York: Greenwillow, 1996. Lilly is so proud of her purse that she disobeys her beloved teacher and plays with it during class. He takes her purse and puts a kind note inside, but Lilly writes her own mean note to the teacher. Lilly learns how to apologize and reconcile.

_____. *Owen,* New York: Greenwillow, 1993. Owen and his parents find a way for him to give up his blanket and keep it at the same time.

_____. Various others.

Hoffman, Mary. *Amazing Grace,* Glenview, IL: Foresman, 1991. In spite of race and gender, Grace proves she can be Peter Pan.

Johnston, Tony. *Sparky and Eddie: The First Day of School*, New York: Scholastic, 1997. Sparky and Eddie are best friends, but their friendship is tested when they begin school and are assigned to different rooms.

Joose, Barbara M. *Mama, Do You Love Me?,* San Francisco: Chronicle, 10th ann. ed., 2001. A mother in the Arctic reassures that she loves her child no matter what.

Lester, Helen. *Hooway for Wodney Wat,* Boston: Houghton, 1999. Wodney Wat, much maligned for his speech impediment, uses his handicap to eliminate a bully from his class.

Lobato, Arcadio. *The Secret of the North Pole,* New York: McGraw, 2003. Peter, a little polar bear, finds a red hat in the snow and returns it to the North Pole, where he learns the secret of how Santa can deliver toys around the world in one night.

Locker, Thomas. *Mountain Dance,* San Diego: Harcourt, 2001. Tells poetically how different kinds of mountains are formed.

Noble, Trinka Hakes. *The Day Jimmy's Boa Ate the Wash*, New York: Penguin, 1980. Jimmy's class takes a field trip to a farm—with Jimmy's boa. The boa causes all kinds of chaos.

_____. Various others.

Parnall, Peter. Various.

Polacco, Patricia. *Pink and Say,* New York: Philomel, 1994. Based on a true story, black Union soldier, Pink, finds injured white soldier Say, takes him home, and, with the help of his mother, nurses Say back to health. They develop a strong friendship. Both are taken to Andersonville where Pink is hanged.

_____. Various others.

Rapunzel. Various eds.

Ryan, Pamela Muñoz. *When Marian Sang*, New York: Scholastic, 2002. True story of Marian Anderson's singing career and the obstacles she faced because of race.

Rylant, Cynthia. *The Great Gracie Chase,* New York: Blue Sky, 2001. Gracie, the dog, liked things to be calm and quiet. She preferred the indoors. But when painters come and disrupt her peace, Gracie takes off out the door.

_____. *When I Was Young in the Mountains,* New York: Puffin, 1993. An autobiographical story about the pleasures of growing up in the mountains.

_____. Various others.

Seuss, Dr. *The Cat in the Hat,* New York: Random, 1957. Brother and sister are bored at home alone until the Cat in the Hat shows them how to have his kind of fun.
_____. Various others.

Soto, Gary. *Too Many Tamales*, New York: Putnam, 1993. Mother and daughters gather to make tamales for the Christmas Eve feast. Maria puts on her mother's wedding ring and loses it. She thinks it is in the tamale dough. Her cousins help look for the ring by eating tamales, only to find the truth.

Stanley, Diane. *Saving Sweetness*, New York: Putnam, 1996. The sheriff, who is telling the story, tells readers how he saved the little orphan, Sweetness. The pictures show the truth.

Steig, William. *Dr. De Soto*, New York: Farrar, 1982. Dentist Dr. De Soto and his wife, both mice, want to help anyone with toothaches. They conceive an ingenious plan to outsmart one of their patients, a fox looking for an easy lunch.
_____. Various others.

Thaler, Mike. *The Cafeteria Lady from the Black Lagoon,* New York: Cartwheel, 1998. Surely the cafeteria lady is evil and the food she serves is bad—but it is not! She's nice and the food is good!

Van Allsburg, Chris. *Jumanji,* Boston: Houghton, 1981. Two children find a board game in the park. They take it home, and when they begin to play, it becomes real, bringing monkeys, a lion, and other dangerous creatures into their home.
_____. Various others.

Viorst, Judith. *I'll Fix Anthony,* Topeka, KS: Bt Bound, 1999. Sibling rivalry at its best, with Anthony's little brother plotting revenge.

Wells, Rosemary. Various.

Wisniewski, David. *Tough Cookie,* New York: HarperCollins, 1999. Tough Cookie lives at the bottom of the cookie jar. When his friend Chips disappears, he determines to get Fingers, the kidnapper. A detective story noir.
_____. *The Secret Knowledge of Grownups*, New York: HarperCollins, 1998. Grownups tell you to do things because they are good for you, but they have secret reasons for imposing their rules.
_____. Various others.

Yolen, Jane. *Owl Moon,* New York: Philomel, 1987. A poetically told story about a father and daughter hiking into the woods at night and calling a great horned owl.

CHAPTER 6

Culminating Activities

A fter your class has studied and practiced the separate elements that comprise a story, help students synthesize their knowledge with the activities that follow.

Book Connections

NCTE 1, 2, 3, 4, 5, 6, 11, 12   Choose a picture book with a particular theme or subject. Then gather books at students' grade level having the same theme or subject. Have each student select one of the grade-level books and read it. Then ask students to write an essay comparing and contrasting the picture book with the grade-level book. Distribute the Book Connections Planning Sheet (Figure 6.1) to help students plan their essays. When they are finished, they will share their essays in small groups. Discuss results with the class, and ask which grade-level books they would recommend to their classmates.

Categorically

NCTE 1, 2, 3, 4, 5, 6, 8, 11, 12   This lesson teaches students summarizing skills by writing annotations and organizing skills by grouping subjects together and putting them in order. It also teaches students that certain types of writing require certain formats, in this case, bibliographic format. Collaborate with lower-grade classroom teachers to find out what units they will be teaching and what supplemental material they might need.

FIGURE 6.1 # Book Connections Planning Sheet

Name(s) _____ Date _____

Complete the blanks below to help you plan your compare and contrast essay.

Title of Picture Book _____

Title of Grade-Level Book _____

List of ways the picture book and grade-level book are the same _____

_____

_____

_____

_____

_____

List of ways the picture book and grade-level book are different _____

_____

_____

_____

_____

I think the (circle one)   picture book   grade-level book
expressed the theme or subject better because

_____

_____

_____

_____

Bring identified subjects to class. Working in groups, students will create subject bibliographies of picture books (and other resources, if desired) to enrich the teachers' units. Students will search available print and Internet resources to find suitable titles. Students will use computer word processing software and correct bibliographic format, following a specified style. They will annotate their entries. The completed bibliographies will be printed for the teachers to keep in their classrooms. They will also be accessible on the computer, either in a file for a particular class or on the school Web page.

Variations

- Brainstorm with students what topics they are interested in and would like to know more about. Record their answers. Choose several by class vote. Working in groups, students will create subject bibliographies of picture books (and other resources, if desired) to further their own learning. Students will search available print and Internet resources to find suitable titles. Students will use computer word processing software and correct bibliographic format, following a specified style. They will annotate their entries. The completed bibliographies will be printed for the classroom. They will also be accessible on the computer, either in a file for a particular class or on the school Web page.

- Use <www.bookadventure.com> to create online reading lists and challenge other readers.

Double Duty

NCTE 1, 2, 3, 4, 5, 6, 7, 11, 12 This assignment will reinforce reading, writing, and other content area lessons. Students will see how one subject area relates to another, and realize a real-life application for their reading and writing skills. Collaborate with classroom teachers in science, social studies, or other subjects. Develop a reading and writing assignment that will fulfill obligations in language arts and another content area. For example, *Stellaluna* by Janell Cannon and related writing activities could be used in science class. Allow students to receive credit in both classes for one assignment, explaining the assessment system for each class. Students will love the efficiency!

Five Star Review

NCTE 1, 3, 4, 5, 6, 8, 11, 12 Choose a picture book and find reviews of the book. Read the book aloud to the class. Ask the class if they have ever heard or read reviews of books or movies. Ask what kind of information is in reviews. A review should tell a little about the plot, setting, characters, theme, and style. It should tell whether or not the author was successful in his or her attempt. With picture books, reviewers also consider how well the art integrates with the text and enhances the story. Reviewers say what they liked and what they did not like and why. The final evaluation (how many stars the book gets) should judge the book as a whole. Re-read the book, this time asking students to think like reviewers. Record comments when you are finished reading. Then read the professional reviews you have found. Do the students agree or disagree with the reviewers?

Distribute the Five Star Review template (Figure 6.2). Working individually or with partners, students will choose a picture book and write a review of it on the template. Share completed templates with the class and display in the classroom or library.

Variations

- Have more advanced students use the Five Star Review template as a planning tool only. They will develop reviews in smooth sentence and paragraph form and share with the class.

- Allow students to read reviews at online Web sites such as <www.Amazon.com> or <www.Barnesandnoble.com>. Read the students' reviews and have students post appropriate ones to the Web sites.

- Publish student reviews in the school newspaper or class newsletter.

Log Dialogue

NCTE 1, 2, 3, 4, 5, 6, 8, 11, 12 This activity allows students to safely share their responses to what they have read. It generates "book talk," encourages clear communication, and helps students see other points of view. Ask students to keep a designated notebook or computer word processing file as a log of responses to their reading. Responses can range from author and illustrator technique to emotional, life applications. Students choose partners with whom they share their logs. Partners write back and forth exchanging responses. Students may keep their logs private, but should be encouraged to comment on their readings.

Log On

NCTE 1, 2, 3, 4, 5, 6, 8, 11, 12 This activity has become a lifelong practice for some students. It allows them to track their reading and helps them remember what they read when. Ask students to keep a reading log that lists the titles, authors, illustrators (if any), main characters, plot summaries, and themes of books they read and the dates they read them. These can take many forms, such as writing in a designated notebook or creating a card file or computer file using word processing or database software. If students need incentives, offer rewards after they have read a certain number of books.

Book vs. Video

NCTE 1, 3, 4, 6, 11, 12 Many picture books have also been made into videos. Choose one title and read the book aloud to the class. Then show the video. Ask students to write an essay comparing and plan their essay. Distribute the Book vs. Video Planning Sheet (Figure 6.3) to help students plan their essay. Ask students to share results in small groups. Take a class vote to see whether students preferred the book or the video.

FIGURE 6.2 **Five Star Review**

Name(s) _____ Date _____

Complete the template below and rate the book by filling in the stars at the bottom of the page. One star is worst, and five stars is best.

Book Title _____

Book Author _____

Book Illustrator _____

What I liked about the story and why _____

_____

_____

What I disliked about the story and why _____

_____

What I liked about the art and why _____

_____

What I disliked about the art and why _____

_____

This book as a whole was (circle one)   successful   unsuccessful   because

_____

_____

I give this book (circle the number of stars you want to give this book)

FIGURE 6.3 # Book vs. Video Planning Sheet

Name(s) _____ Date _____

Complete the blanks below to help you plan your compare and contrast essay.

Title of Book and Video _____

List of ways the book and video are the same _____

_____

_____

_____

_____

List of ways the book and video are different _____

_____

_____

_____

_____

_____

I liked the (circle one)   book   video
better because _____

_____

_____

_____

_____

_____

In Any Language

NCTE 1, 3, 4, 9, 10, 11, 12 Find adult volunteers who know languages other than English, including American Sign Language. Ask the volunteers to read aloud a picture book in their languages. Have students extract the story from picture context, vocal clues, and facial expression. Student volunteers will tell or write the story they have interpreted based on context clues. Then, as the adult reader tells the story in English, students should compare their versions with the one that was told. Ask the volunteers to teach students to write a few key words in their languages. Sponsor a multicultural day and have students recite their stories.

Read-Aloud Fun

NCTE 1, 2, 3, 4, 5, 6, 11, 12 To truly appreciate language, read stories aloud. Have students choose picture books to read aloud. (They may also choose to read their original stories.) Introduce tips from the *Read-Aloud Handbook* by Jim Trelease. Students will practice with partners first and then read their stories to the class. Coordinate with teachers in lower grades to have students read stories to younger students. Ask the principal if students can read a story over the intercom. Students may also read at preschools, parent events, nursing homes, and other community venues.

Acting Out

NCTE 1, 2, 3, 4, 5, 6, 11, 12 Working in small groups, students will choose a picture book favorite and rewrite it in script form. They will dramatize the story for the rest of the class, for other classes, or for special events. The story can be performed as a full dramatization, as Reader's Theater, or as a choral reading. (For more on Reader's Theater and choral reading see <www.scriptsforschools.com> and <www.aaronshep.com>.)

Story Power

NCTE 3, 4, 5, 6, 11, 12 Each student will take one of his or her original stories (perhaps one written for a previous lesson) and create a PowerPoint® slide presentation. Collaborate with the technology teacher, who will give a lesson on the software basics and assist students as they work on their projects. Students will show their presentations to the class, to other classes, or to special event audiences. The presentations may also be posted on the school Web page.

It Pays to Advertise

NCTE 1, 2, 3, 4, 5, 6, 8, 11, 12 Ask students to create a TV ad for a book. Working in groups, students will choose a picture book they want to promote. They will determine the book's strong points. They may look at book reviews as research. They will write 30-second or 60-second ad copy, and videotape it. Students will play their ad for the class or post it to the school Web site. Your local TV station may also play ads as public service announcements.

Puzzlemania

NCTE 1, 3, 4, 5, 6, 8, 11, 12 Working with partners, students will choose a picture book and create one or more puzzles based on the book. Puzzles include jigsaws, crosswords, word finds, anagrams, or any other puzzle students enjoy. Students can create them using paper and pencil or using puzzle creating computer software. Puzzle software, such as A2Z Word Puzzler, is available free at <www.shareware.com>. Puzzles can be made available on the computer or as reproducibles for the entire class, or other classes, to do.

Who Wrote It?

NCTE 1, 3, 5, 6, 7, 8, 11, 12 Ask students to write reports about picture book authors and illustrators. Each student will choose an author or illustrator and use library and online resources to learn more about the author or illustrator. Online information is available at these Web sites, as well as at publishers' Web sites:

AuthorChats. Home Page

Matulka, Denise I. *Picturing Books : A Web Site About Picture Books*
    <http://picturingbooks.imaginarylands.org/>

SCBWI Member Links. 2002. Society of Children's Book Writers and Illustrators
    <www.scbwi.org/links/mem_links.htm>

Students may also email authors and illustrators with specific questions. Students will present their papers to the class.

Author, Author

NCTE 4, 5, 6, 8. 11, 12 Students have learned and practiced writing the various story elements. They have learned about picture book illustration. Now have them put it all together by asking them to write and illustrate their own original picture books. They may use paper and general art supplies or computer software. When they are finished, they will share their books with the class and with other classes.

Variations

- Rather than having each student make a picture book, ask each student to contribute a short story for a class book. The finished book will be printed and kept in the classroom or library.

- Rather than having each student make a picture book, ask each student to contribute a short story, essay, or poem for publication in a class magazine. The magazine could be printed or could be on the school Web page as an e-zine.

Picture Books Cited

Aardema, Verna. *Borreguita and the Coyote*.

Ackerman, Karen. *Song and Dance Man*.

Aesop's Fables.

Agran, Rick. *Pumpkin Shivaree*.

Allard, Harry. *Miss Nelson Is Missing*.

Altman, Linda Jacobs. *The Legend of Freedom Hill*.

Andersen, Hans Christian. *Ugly Duckling*.

Andreae, Giles. *Giraffes Can't Dance*.

Arnold, Katya. *Baba Yaga: A Russian Folktale*.

Bang, Molly. *Ten, Nine, Eight*.

_____. *When Sophie Gets Angry—Really, Really Angry*.

Barner, Bob. *Parade Day*.

Baylor, Byrd. *Everybody Needs a Rock*.

_____. *If You Are a Hunter of Fossils*.

_____. *I'm in Charge of Celebrations*.

_____. *The Table Where the Rich People Sit*.

_____. *The Way to Start a Day*.

Beames, Margaret. *Night Cat*.

Bearden, Romare. *Li'l Dan the Drummer Boy*.

Berger, Barbara Helen. *All the Way to Lhasa*.

Birnbaum, Abe. *Green Eyes*.

Briggs, Raymond. *The Snowman*.

Brown, Marcia. *Once a Mouse....*

Brown, Margaret Wise. *The Runaway Bunny*.

Browne, Anthony. *The Piggybook*.

Bunting, Eve. *Fly Away Home*.

_____. *Smoky Night*.

_____. *The Wednesday Surprise*.

_____. *A Turkey for Thanksgiving*.

Burton, Virginia Lee. *The Little House*.

Buscaglia, Leo. *The Fall of Freddie the Leaf*.

Cannon, Janell. *Stellaluna*.

Carmi, Giora. *A Circle of Friends*.

Casler, Leigh. *The Boy Who Dreamed of an Acorn*.

Cinderella.

Clifton, Lucille. *Everett Anderson's Friend*.

Cohen, Miriam. *Will I Have a Friend?*

Cole, Joanna. *Bony-Legs*.

Cooney, Barbara. *Chanticleer and the Fox*.

Coursen, Valerie. *Mordant's Wish*.

Cronin, Doreen. *Click, Clack, Moo: Cows that Type*.

_____. *Diary of a Worm*.

Cutler, Jane. *The Cello of Mr. O*.

Daly, Niki. *Jamela's Dress*.

Day, Alexander. *Carl Goes Shopping*.

_____. *Carl's Afternoon in the Park*.

_____. *Carl's Birthday*.

_____. *Carl's Masquerade*.

_____. *Follow Carl!*

De Felice, Cynthia. *Old Granny and the Bean Thief*.

DeGroat, Diane. *Roses Are Pink, Your Feet Really Stink*.

Demi. *The Empty Pot*.

DePaola, Tomie. *Nana Upstairs & Nana Downstairs*.

_____. *Oliver Button is a Sissy*.

_____. *Strega Nona*.

Diakite, Baba Wague. *The Hatseller and the Monkeys*

Doner, Kim. *Buffalo Dreams*.

Dorros, Arthur. *Abuela*.

Dyer, Sarah. *Five Little Fiends*.

Eduar, Gilles. *Jooka Saves the Day*.

Egan, Tim. *Metropolitan Cow*.

Ehlert, Lois. *Top Cat*.

Elliott, Laura Malone. *Hunter's Best Friend at School*.

Ernst, Lisa Campbell. *Zinnia and Dot*.

Everitt, Betsy. *Mean Soup*.

Falconer, Ian. *Olivia*.

Feelings, Muriel. *Moja Means One*.

Felix, Monique. *The Alphabet*.

_____. *The Wind*.

Fine, Edith Hope. *Under the Lemon Moon*.

Fisher, Valerie. *My Big Sister*.

Fleischman, Paul. *Weslandia*.

Fleming, Denise. *Buster*.

Gackenback, Dick. *Claude the Dog*.

Galdone, Paul. *Henny Penny*.

_____. *The Magic Porridge Pot*.

_____. *The Three Bears*.

Gantos, Jack. *Rotten Ralph's Rotten Romance*.

Gerstein, Mordicai. *The Man Who Walked Between the Towers*.

_____. *Mountains of Tibet*.

Goble, Paul. *The Girl Who Loved Wild Horses*.

_____. *Iktomi and the Boulder*.

Graham, Bob. *Crusher is Coming*.

Graves, Keith. *Frank Was a Monster Who Wanted to Dance*.

Gray, Libba Moore. *My Mama had a Dancing Heart*.

Greenfield, Eloise. *Me and Neesie*.

_____. *She Come Bringing Me That Little Baby Girl*.

Haas, Jesse. *Busybody Brandy*.

Haley, Gail E. *A Story! A Story!*

Havill, Juanita. *Jamaica Tag-Along*.

Hazen, Barbara. *Tight Times*.

Henkes, Kevin. *Chrysanthemum.*

_____. *Julius, the Baby of the World.*

_____. *Lilly's Purple Plastic Purse.*

_____. *Owen.*

Hest, Amy. *When Jessie Came Across the Sea.*

Hoban, Lillian. *Arthur's Great Big Valentine.*

Hoban, Russell. *Bread and Jam for Frances.*

Hoestalandt, Jo. *Star of Fear, Star of Hope.*

Hoffman, Mary. *Amazing Grace.*

Hort, Lenny. *How Many Stars in the Sky?*

Houston, Gloria. *My Great-Aunt Arizona.*

Howard, Arthur. *Serious Trouble.*

Hutchins, Pat. *Changes, Changes.*

Isadora, Rachel. *Ben's Trumpet.*

_____. *Max.*

Jackson, Isaac. *Somebody's New Pajamas.*

Johnston, Tony. *Alice Nizzy Nazzy: The Witch of Santa Fe.*

_____. *Sparky and Eddie: The First Day of School.*

Joose, Barbara M. *Mama, Do You Love Me?*

Joyce, William. *Santa Calls.*

Kasza, Keiko. *Wolf's Chicken Stew.*

Keats, Ezra Jack. *Goggles.*

_____. *The Snowy Day.*

_____. *Whistle for Willie.*

Kimmel, Eric. *Hershel and the Hanukkah Goblins.*

Kraus, Robert. *Leo the Late Bloomer.*

Krensky, Stephen. *My Teacher's Secret Life.*

Kvasnosky, Laura McGee. *Zelda and Ivy.*

Lester, Helen. *Hooway for Wodney Wat.*

_____. *Tacky the Penguin.*

Lester, Julius. *Black Cowboy, Wild Horses.*

_____. *John Henry.*

Lewin, Betsy. *What's the Matter, Habibi?*

Lewin, Hugh. *Jafta's Father.*

Lionni, Leo. *Alexander and the Wind-Up Mouse.*

_____. *Frederick.*

_____. *Swimmy.*

Lipkind, William and Nicolas Mordivinoff. *Finders Keepers.*

Lobato, Arcadio. *The Secret of the North Pole.*

Lobel, Arnold. *Fables.*

_____. *Frog and Toad Are Friends.*

_____. *Frog and Toad Together.*

_____. *On Market Street.*

Locker, Thomas. *Mountain Dance.*

_____. *Walking with Henry.*

_____. *Where the River Begins.*

London, Jonathan. *Froggy Gets Dressed.*

_____. *Froggy Plays Soccer.*

Low, Joseph. *Mice Twice.*

Marshall, James. *George and Martha.*

_____. *Yummers!*

Martin, Jacqueline Griggs. *Snowflake Bentley.*

Mayer, Mercer. *A Boy, a Dog, and a Frog.*

_____. *A Boy, A Dog, a Frog, and a Friend.*

_____. *Frog Goes to Dinner.*

_____. *Frog on his Own.*

_____. *Frog, Where Are You?*

_____. *Liza Lou and the Yeller Belly Swamp.*

_____. *One Frog Too Many.*

McAllister, Angela. *The Little Blue Rabbit.*

McCarty, Peter. *Hondo and Fabian.*

McCloskey, Robert. *Make Way for Ducklings.*

McCourt, Lisa. *I Miss You, Stinky Face.*

McCully, Emily Arnold. *Mirette on the High Wire.*

McKee, David. *Elmer.*

McKissack, Patricia. *Flossie and the Fox.*

McLerran, Alice. *Roxaboxen.*

McPhail, David. *Farm Morning.*

_____. *Pig Pig Grows Up.*

Meddaugh, Susan. *Hog-Eye.*

Mitchell, Lori. *Different Just Like Me.*

Mora, Pat. *Tomas and the Library Lady.*

Moss, Marissa. *True Heart.*

Munsch, Robert. *Love You Forever.*

Ness, Evaline. *Sam, Bangs and Moonshine.*

Noble, Trinka Hakes. *The Day Jimmy's Boa Ate the Wash.*

_____. *Meanwhile, Back at the Ranch.*

Numeroff, Laura. *If You Take a Mouse to School.*

Nye, Naomi Shihab. *Baby Radar.*

_____. *Sitti's Secrets.*

Polacco, Patricia. *Pink and Say.*

Potter, Beatrix. *The Tale of Peter Rabbit.*

Priceman, Marjorie. *How to Make an Apple Pie and See the World.*

Prigger, Mary Skillings. *Aunt Minnie McGranahan.*

Rahaman, Vashanti. *Read for Me, Mama.*

Rapunzel.

Raschka, Chris. *Ring! Yo?*

Rathman, Peggy. *Officer Buckle and Gloria.*

Rey, H.A *Curious George.*

Ringold, Faith. *Tar Beach.*

Rohmann, Eric. *My Friend Rabbit.*

_____. *Time Flies.*

Ryan, Pamela Muñoz. *When Marian Sang.*

Rylant, Cynthia. *The Great Gracie Chase.*

_____. *Henry and Mudge.*

_____. *When I Was Young in the Mountains.*

San Souci, Robert D. *The Faithful Friend.*

_____. *A Weave of Words.*

Say, Allen. *Grandfather's Journey.*

_____. *Stranger in the Mirror.*

Sceiszka, Jon. *The True Story of the Three Little Pigs.*

Schachner, Judith Byron. *The Grannyman.*

_____. *Skippyjon Jones.*

Scheffler, Ursel. *Who Has Time for Little Bear?*

Seeger, Pete. *Abiyoyo.*

Sendak, Maurice. *Pierre.*

_____. *Where the Wild Things Are.*

Seuling, Barbara. *Winter Lullaby.*

Seuss, Dr. *The Cat in the Hat.*

_____. *How the Grinch Stole Christmas.*

Shannon, David. *David Goes to School.*

_____. *No, David*

Shannon, George. *Dance Away.*

_____. *Lizard's Song.*

Sharmat, Marjorie Wienman. *Gila Monsters Meet You at the Airport.*

Shulevitz, Uri. *Snow.*

_____. *The Treasure.*

Silverstein, Shel. *The Giving Tree.*

Sis, Peter. *Madlenka.*

Smothers, Ethel Footman. *The Hard-Times Jar.*

Snyder, Dianne. *The Boy of the Three Year Nap.*

Soto, Gary. *Chato's Kitchen.*

_____. *Too Many Tamales.*

Stanley, Diane. *Saving Sweetness.*

Steig, William. *Dr. De Soto.*

_____. *Sylvester and the Magic Pebble.*

Steptoe, John. *Stevie.*

Stevens, Janet. *Coyote Steals the Blanket.*

_____. *Tops and Bottoms.*

Stewart, Sarah. *The Gardner.*

Tamar, Erika. *The Garden of Happiness.*

Thaler, Mike. *The Cafeteria Lady from the Black Lagoon.*

Trivizas, Eugene. *The Three Little Wolves and the Big Bad Pig.*

Turkle, Brinton. *Do Not Open.*

Van Allsburg, Chris. *Jumanji.*

_____. *The Polar Express.*

_____. *The Sweetest Fig.*

Viorst, Judith. *I'll Fix Anthony.*

Ward, Lynd. *The Biggest Bear.*

Weitzman, Jacqueline Preiss and Robin Preiss Glasser. *You Can't Take a Balloon into the Metropolitan Museum.*

Wellington, Monica. *Night City*.

Wells, Rosemary. *Bunny Cakes*.

_____. *Hazel's Amazing Mother*.

_____. *Yoko*.

Wiesner, David. *Sector 7*.

_____. *Tuesday*.

Williams, Suzanne. *Library Lil*.

Williams, Vera B. *A Chair for my Mother*.

Williams, Vera B. and Jennifer Williams. *Stringbean's Trip to the Shining Sea*.

Wisniewski, David. *Golem*.

_____. *Tough Cookie*.

_____. *The Secret Knowledge of Grownups*.

Wood, Audrey. *King Bidgood's in the Bathtub*.

_____. *The Napping House*.

Wood, Douglas. *Old Turtle*.

Woodruff, Elvira. *The Memory Coat*.

Wright, Betty Ren. *The Blizzard*.

Yolan, Jane. *The Musicians of Bremen*.

_____. *Owl Moon*.

Yorinks, Arthur. *Hey, Al*.

Young, Ed. *Lon Po Po: A Red-Riding Hood Story from China*.

_____. *Seven Blind Mice*.

Zelinsky, Paul O. *Rapunzel*.

Zemach, Harve. *The Judge: An Untrue Tale*.

Zemach, Margot. *It Could Always Be Worse: A Yiddish Tale*.

Selected List of Works Consulted

Books

Alphin, Elaine Marie. *Creating Characters Kids Will Love*, Cincinnati: Writer's Digest, 2000.

Amoss, Berthe and Eric Suben. *The Children's Writer's Reference*, Cincinnati: Writer's Digest, 1999.

Benedict, Susan and Lenore Carlisle, Eds. *Beyond Words: Picture Books for Older Readers and Writers*, Portsmouth, NH: Heinemann, 1992.

Bishop, Kay. *Connecting Libraries with Classrooms: the Curricular Roles of the Media Specialist*, Worthington, OH: Linworth, 2003.

Buzzeo, Toni. *Collaborating to Meet Standards: Teacher/Librarian Partnerships for K-6*, Worthington, OH: Linworth, 2002.

_____. *Collaborating to Meet Standards: Teacher/Librarian Partnerships for 7-12*, Worthington, OH: Linworth. 2002.

Children's Writer's and Illustrator's Market, Cincinnati: Writer's Digest, 2001. (This is an annual publication. Quote from this ed.)

Cleaver, Pamela. *Writing a Children's Book*, Oxford, UK: How To, 2000. OP

Culham, Ruth. *Picturebooks: an Annotated Bibliography with Activities for Teaching Writing*, Portland, OR: Northwest Regional Educational Laboratory, Fifth ed., 1998.

Curriculum Connections: Picture Books in Grades 3 and Up, Worthington, OH: Linworth, 1999.

Ellis, Sarah. *From Reader to Writer: Teaching Writing Through Classic Children's Books*, Berkeley, CA: Publishers Group West, 2000.

Forte, Imogene. *Using Favorite Picture Books to Stimulate Discussion and Encourage Critical Thinking*, Nashville: Incentive, 1995.

Hall, Susan. *Using Picture Storybooks to Teach Literary Devices*, Phoenix: Oryx, 1994.

Harms, Jeanne McLain. *Picture Books to Enhance the Curriculum*, New York: Wilson, 1996.

Information Power: Building Partnerships for Learning, Chicago: ALA, 1998.

Kurstedt, Rosanne and Maria Koutras. *Teaching Writing with Picture Books as Models: Lessons and Strategies for Using*, New York: Scholastic, 2000.

Lamb, Nancy. *The Writer's Guide to Crafting Stories for Children*, Cincinnati: Writer's Digest, 2001.

Macrorie, Ken. *Telling Writing*, Portsmouth, NH: Boynton/Cook, 4th ed., 1985.

McCutcheon, Marc. *The Writer's Digest Sourcebook for Building Believable Characters*, Cincinnati: Writer's Digest, 2000.

Mealy, Virginia. *From Reader to Writer: Creative Writing in the Middle Grades Using Picture Books*, Metuchen, NJ: Scarecrow, 1986. OP

Nespeca, Sue McCleaf and Joan B. Reeve. *Picture Books Plus: 100 Extension Activities in Art, Drama, Music, Math, and Science*, Chicago: ALA, 2003.

Roberts, Joyce and Tammy Watanabe Hall. *Using Picture Books with Older Students, Book 1*, San Luis Obispo, CA: Dandy Lion Publications, 1995.

Roser, Nancy L. and Miriam G. Martinez, eds. *Book Talk and Beyond*, Newark, DE:

International Reading Assoc., 1995.

Saunders, Sheryl Lee. *Look—and Learn!: Using Picture Books in Grades Five through Eight,* Portsmouth, NH: Heinemann, 1999.

Scholastic Children's Dictionary, NY: Scholastic, 2002.

Scholastic Dictionary of Idioms, NY: Scholastic, 1998.

Stephens, Claire Gatrell. *Picture This! Using Picture Story Books for Character Education in the Classroom*, Westport, CT: Libraries Unlimited, 2004.

Strunk, William, Jr. *The Elements of Style*, Needham Heights, MA: Pearson, 4th ed., 1999.

Thomason, Tommy and Carol York. *Absolutely Write! Teaching the Craft Elements of Writing*, Norwood, MA: Christopher-Gordon, 2002.

Trelease, Jim. *The Read-Aloud Handbook*, Topeka, KS: Bt Bound, 5th ed., 2001.

Weissman. Annie. *Expand and Enrich Reading: Reading and Writing Activities*, Worthington, OH: Linworth, 2003.

Zinsser, William K. *On Writing Well*, New York: HarperResource, 25th ann. ed., 2001.

Personal Interviews

Kleven, Julia. Personal interview. 28 Nov. 2003.

Noland, Janet. Personal interview. 28 Nov. 2003.

Web Sites

Amazon.com. Home Page. 2004 Amazon.com. 1 Apr. 2004 <www.amazon.com>. Book and product seller. Provides complete publishing information and reviews.

American Assn. of School Librarians. Home Page. 2004. American Library Assn. 4 Apr. 2004 <www.ala.org/aasl>.

American Library Assn. Home Page. 2004. American Library Assn. 1 Apr. 2004 <www.ala.org>.

AuthorChats. Home Page. 2003. 1 Apr. 2004 <http://www.authorchats.com/>. Author chats. As of this writing, only archived chats are available, as the server is being moved.

Barnesandnoble.com. Home Page. 2004. Barnes and Noble. 1 Apr. 2004 <www.barnesandnoble.com>. Book and product seller. Provides complete publishing information and reviews.

Berger, Barbara Helen. Home Page. 1 Apr. 2004. <http://bhberger.coml>.

Book Adventure. 2004. Sylvan Learning Center. 1 Apr. 2004 <www.bookadventure.com>. Offers opportunity to create book lists, challenge other classes or families, take quizzes. Sections for kids, parents, and teachers.

Education World. 2003. EdMin.com. 24 Jun 2004 <http://www.educationworld.com/>. A total education site with lesson plans, rubrics, articles, search engine, professional development suggestions, job openings, and more.

Hurst, Carol and Rebecca Otis. *Carol Hurst's Children's Literature Site*. 1999. 1 Apr. 2004. <www.carolhurst.com>. Has book reviews, library and teaching ideas, monthly newsletter.

International Reading Association Home Page. 2004. International Reading Assn. 1 Apr. 2004 <www.ira.org>.

Matulka, Denise I. *Picturing Books : A Web Site About Picture Books.* Home Page. 2002. 1 Apr. 2004 <http://picturingbooks.imaginarylands.org>. Lots of information about picture book construction, art, writing, authors, and illustrators.

Monster. 2004. 1 Apr. 2004 <www.monster.com>. Job information site.

My Hero Project. Home Page. 1 Apr. 2004 < http://www.myhero.com/myhero/>. Students learn about real-life heroes in various categories including writers, add their own hero stories, and write to the Forum section. Lesson plans and stories for teachers. May be useful for character discussion.

National Council of Teachers of English Home Page. 2004. National Council of Teachers of English. 1 Apr. 2004 <www.ncte.org>.

National Council of Teachers of English. *Standards for the English Language Arts.* 2004. National Council of Teachers of English. 1 Apr. 2004 <www.ncte.org/about/over/standards/110846.htm>.

Heffner, Christopher L. "Chapter 3: Personality Development, Section 2: Motor and Cognitive Development," *Psychology 101.* 2004. AllPsych ONLINE. 28 Mar. 2004. <http://allpsych.com/psychology101/development.html>.

SCBWI Member Links. 2002. Society of Children's Book Writers and Illustrators. 1 Apr. 2004 < http://www.scbwi.org/links/mem_links.htm>. Links to home pages of children's authors and illustrators.

Scholastic, Inc. *Character Education by the Book.* 2001. 1 Apr. 2004 <http://teacher.scholastic.com/professional/todayschild/charactered.htm>. Contains information and lesson plans on character education and values, which could be used with theme discussion.

Shareware.com. 1 Apr. 2004. CNET Networks, Inc. 1 Apr. 2004 <www.shareware.com>. Offers free downloads of shareware software. Good for making puzzles and word games.

Shepherd, Aaron. *Aaron Shepherd's Home Page.* 1 Apr. 2004 <www.aaronshep.com>. Offers information about Reader's Theater, choral reading, writing and publishing for kids and adults.

Walker, Lois. *Scripts For Schools.* 1 Apr. 2004 <www.scriptsforschools.com>. Provides some free Reader's Theater and choral reading scripts, as well as commercial scripts. Gives information about Readers Theater and choral reading.

Warlick, David. 2004. *Landmarks for Schools.* The Landmark Project. 24 Jun 2004 <http://www.landmark-project.com>. An education site that contains building blocks for rubrics, citations, and Web sites, as well as articles and teaching ideas.

Westing Game: Notes. Cooperative Children's Book Center. School of Education. University of Wisconsin-Madison. 1 Apr. 2004 <www.soemadison.wisc.edu/ccbc/wisauth/raskin/notes.htm> Working notes about the *Westing Game* by author Ellen Raskin.

Index